More than meets the eye

More than meets the eye

A closer look at paintings in
the National Gallery

MICHAEL CASSIN

NATIONAL GALLERY PUBLICATIONS
LONDON

Distributed by Yale University Press

National Gallery Publications Ltd.
© Michael Cassin and The National Gallery 1987
Reprinted 1990, 1994

British Library Cataloguing in Publication Data

  Cassin, Michael
    More than meets the eye.
    1. Painting—History
    I. Title II. National Gallery
    759   ND50

    ISBN 0 947645 03 9

Printed by Lawrence-Allen (Colour Printers) Ltd., Weston-super-Mare.

Cover illustration: Sassetta (1392? – 1450)
The Legend of the Wolf of Gubbio (detail)

Contents ———————————

Foreword———————————

This book arises directly out of the author's almost daily experience in meeting and talking to – and also listening to – younger visitors to the National Gallery. And to that wide, I hope widening, public, his book is primarily addressed.

At the same time, it can usefully be read by anyone who has felt some stirrings of interest in looking at paintings and has longed to know more generally about how they come into existence, why they may look as they do, and what the functions of a great art gallery are.

Michael Cassin manages to give very positive answers to such questions, in admirably clear language. Rightly, he is not afraid of considering basic aspects of a subject that can seem forbiddingly abstruse and which is certainly complex.

What his book offers, above all, is a friendly hand and some encouraging words to guide people to enter more freely and uninhibitedly into the endlessly enjoyable visual world created by paintings. There is always, as his title aptly conveys, more than meets the eye in such work – which is why the process of looking is never-ending. Yet all of us, sooner or later, need some guidance on that long journey.

This book is the product of enthusiasm, knowledge and experience, and I think in all those ways it typifies the Education Department of the Gallery, in whose activities the author, as a Schools Officer, plays a significant part.

Michael Levey
DIRECTOR 1973–86

1 Jan van der Straet
(Stradanus) (1532–1605)
An Artist's Studio (detail)

I: MAKING PICTURES

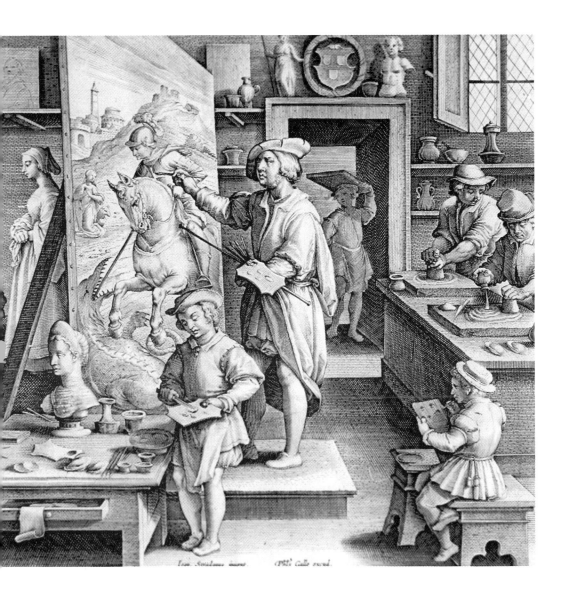

Ioan. Stradanus inuent.   Phls Galle excud.

Composition

M any people have a very romantic idea of how artists work. They imagine them waiting for inspiration to strike, like some kind of benign lightning bolt. When this happens they are supposed to rush to their studios and paint feverishly until the mood passes or the work is finished.

The composition of a painting may sometimes appear fully formed in an artist's imagination, but more often it has to be thought out and designed. A painter may do this before he touches a brush or a canvas, or he may rely on his experience and allow the composition to develop as he works. In either

2 Attributed to Jacopo di Cione
(active 1362, died 1398/1400)
*The Coronation of the
Virgin, with Adoring Saints*

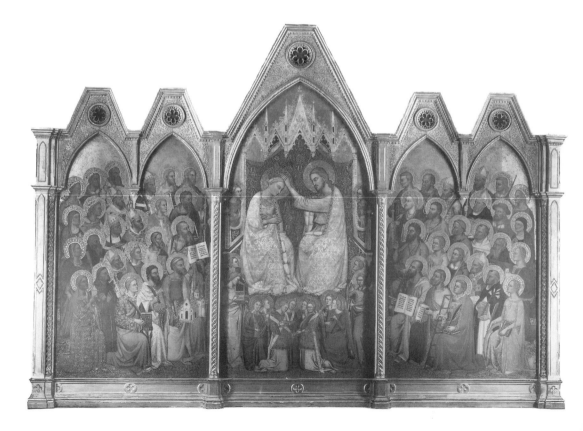

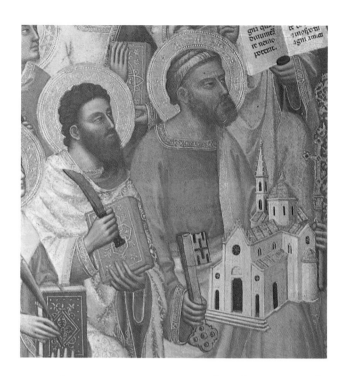

3 Detail of St Peter from
The Coronation of the Virgin

case, the process is more complex than we might suppose from looking at the end result.

The *Coronation of the Virgin* [2], an altarpiece attributed to Jacopo di Cione, was originally intended to decorate the high altar of a church in Florence. It was a large painting incorporating a number of small panels in addition to the three main ones shown here. The most important people in the painting, Jesus and Mary, are shown in the centre, sitting on an ornate throne, higher and larger than everyone else. The saints on either side may be identified by the clothes they wear and the objects they carry. For example, St Peter (3) holds in his right hand the key to the Kingdom of Heaven, which is his particular symbol. St Peter was the patron saint of the church for which the painting was made (he holds a model of it on his knee), so he occupies a more prominent position than someone like St Gregory who appears in the same panel, in the middle of the third row. The saints direct their attention towards Jesus and Mary, but some of the angels in the heavenly choir look at the congregation, as if to form a link between the holy people in the painting and the ordinary people in church.

The altarpiece would have been designed specifically for its original location above the altar in a candle-lit church, where only the clergy would have been able to get as close to it as we can today. In this setting the abundant gold leaf would have caught and reflected the flickering candle-light, and each saint's head would have been surrounded by a magical golden glow. This special effect must have greatly impressed superstitious visitors to the church in the fourteenth century.

The composition may seem a bit too symmetrical to us now but it has the great benefit of being clear and legible. Most of the saints are easy to see and to identify, their poses and gestures remind visitors to the church that they ought to kneel before Jesus and His Mother. The positioning of the figures within the painting shows us how important they are, and leads our eyes to the people who are the centre of attention. This kind of expressive design is what composition is all about.

The composition of Piero della Francesca's *Baptism of Christ* (4) is very balanced and for the most part completely static. Only the man undressing on the right suggests movement of any kind, and even he seems to be frozen in mid action, as if time has stood still for a moment. This static balance is not accidental. It is the result of a design that demonstrates the artist's strong interest in mathematics. The composition has been planned according to a system of proportion that was first developed by the ancient Greeks. It became popular during the fifteenth century in Italy, when artists, among others, again became interested in the classical past. It is known as the 'Golden Section'.

You may not be a mathematician and neither am I, but we may be able to understand the system fairly easily if we examine Piero's painting. The horizontal line formed by the Dove and the adjacent cloud divides the panel in two. If we call the height of the whole panel 'A', the distance between the Dove and the base 'B' and the distance between the Dove and the top 'C', then A:B equals B:C.

4 Piero della Francesca (c.1415/20–1492) *The Baptism of Christ*

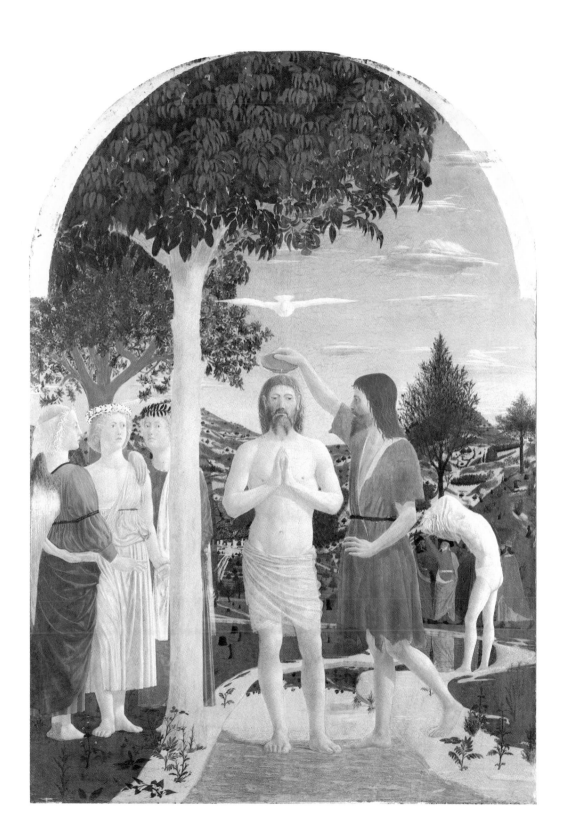

The Golden Section was thought to be the perfect ratio because it involved only three measurements. If you look carefully you may notice that it has been used elsewhere in Piero's painting. In fact once you know about it, you may begin to see similar proportions all over the place.

Of course Piero's *Baptism* is very much more than just a mathematical exercise. The artist has also created a convincing illusion of depth and sculptural solidity; he has illustrated a sacred story in a clear and comprehensible way; and he has created a painting that is harmonious and very beautiful.

It is obvious that Piero's painting has been very carefully designed. The artist may have made studies of the landscape and of each individual figure, and it is likely that he produced one final drawing in which all the main elements of the composition were included. Many painters of the fifteenth and sixteenth centuries worked in this way. For example, Raphael's *Allegory ('Vision of a Knight')* (5) was preceded by a drawing (6) in which he fixed the positions of the figures and some of the details of the landscape, and indicated the highlights and the main areas of shadow. Only the colours are absent.

5 Raphael (1483–1520)
An Allegory

6 Cartoon for *An Allegory*

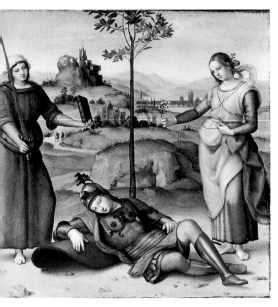

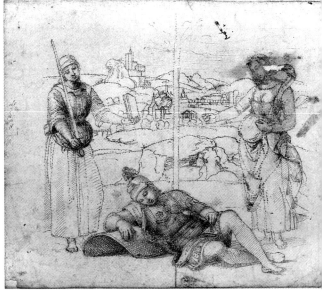

6

The drawing is exactly the same size as the finished painting. This was to make it easier for the artist to transfer the design from the paper to the panel on which the painting was to be executed. If you look carefully you should be able to see that tiny holes have been made in the paper, following the main lines of the drawing. Powdered charcoal would have been dusted over the paper while it rested on the panel, so that the dark powder filtered through the holes, carrying the design onto the panel's surface. This kind of preparatory drawing is called a 'cartoon', a name which derives from the Italian word 'cartone' literally meaning 'stiff paper'.

Of course, there are many other methods of transferring a design, but some artists continued to use full-sized cartoons until well into the nineteenth century. When artists exhibited their designs for paintings to decorate the new Houses of Parliament in the last century comic parodies of the entries were published in the magazine *Punch*. It was this apparently that led to such comic drawings being called cartoons from then on.

Rubens made preparatory studies for many of his paintings but there were times too when he allowed his compositions to develop as he worked on them. In *'The Watering Place'* (7) he seems to have started with a small panel on which he painted some of the shaded area around the pool. He then added strips of wood to all sides of the picture and extended the composition, altering the lighting as he did so. The finished painting looks so natural that it is difficult to imagine it was not done directly from nature.

Having extended the size of the panel Rubens had room to include a greater range of atmospheric effects and also some details of pastoral life. In the final version we can see the sun through a clearing sky on the left-hand side, while on the right, dark clouds hang ominously above the trees. In the foreground horses and cattle drink at the water's edge, a calf nuzzles its mother, a girl carries water in a bucket and balances a large pitcher on her head, and a young boy relaxes in the shade while everyone else is working. Rubens' picture is, of course, a skilfully constructed work of art but the overgrown woodland is so

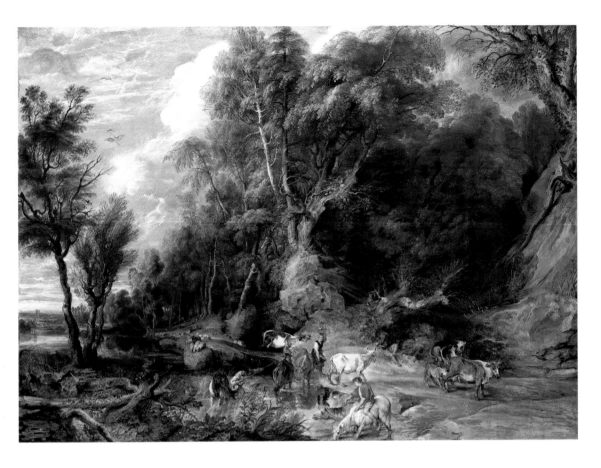

convincingly painted that it looks unstudied and completely natural.

Degas also wanted some of his compositions to look unstudied, as though he was peeping at his models through a key-hole without their knowledge. The composition of the picture *Combing the Hair* (8) may look accidental but in fact it was carefully worked out in a number of sketches and variants. The table bridges the space between the spectator and the women portrayed. The unconventional pose of the seated figure, whose body is stretched across the canvas, is emphasized by the daring use of the same red for the dress, hair, curtain and background. The painting may be unfinished but it shows that by means of careful planning Degas was able to achieve the unstudied effect he desired.

7 Rubens (1577–1640)
'The Watering Place'

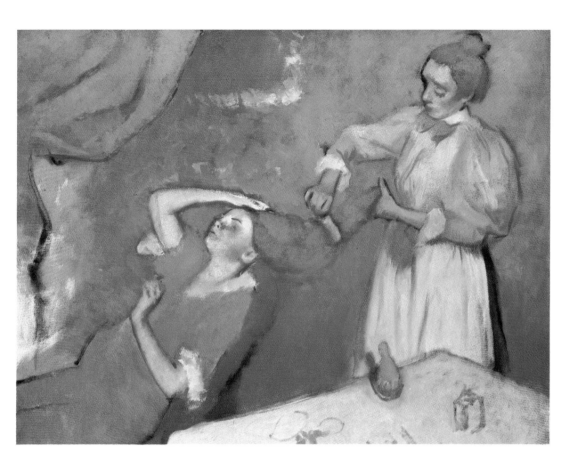

8 Degas (1834–1917)
Combing the Hair

From these few examples we can see that paintings are rarely accidental images: the artist is always in control. Whether he invents a composition before he starts to paint or develops it as he paints, the final design is almost always the product of a series of decisions. Inspiration may be less important to an artist than experience and hard work.

Light and Shade

In the theatre spotlights direct the attention of the audience and help it to pick out the star of the show from the rest of the cast. In the cinema long shadows and dark silhouettes have been used so often to suggest mystery that it is almost a cliché to do this nowadays. In the physical world light and shadows perform more fundamental functions. They tell us about shapes and surfaces, about the bulk and solidity of objects and people. In paintings artists have used contrasts of light and shade – called 'chiaroscuro', which literally means 'light–dark' – to create effects similar to all those mentioned above.

The *Virgin and Child* by Masaccio (9) shows Mary, the Mother of Jesus, sitting on a throne, with her infant son and four attendant angels. It was painted around 1426 as the centre part of an altarpiece. The arched top and gold background are traditional, as is the colour of the Virgin's cloak. What is less traditional is the way in which the artist has used variations in tone to suggest the weight and solidity of the figures and the throne. We know we are looking at a flat surface but the figures seem as three-dimensional as they would if they were pieces of sculpture bathed in light. The sides of the throne project towards us and the patterns on the base catch the light and recede into shadow as if they were carved rather than painted.

Of course, Masaccio was not the first artist to paint imitations of carved stone. A hundred years earlier Giotto had produced a series of frescoes in the Arena Chapel in Padua that includes a number of figures painted in monochrome to look like marble statues. The same technique, known as 'grisaille', was used by Hans Memlinc in his painting of *The Virgin and Child with Saints and Donors* (10).

9 Masaccio (1401–1428?)
The Virgin and Child

10

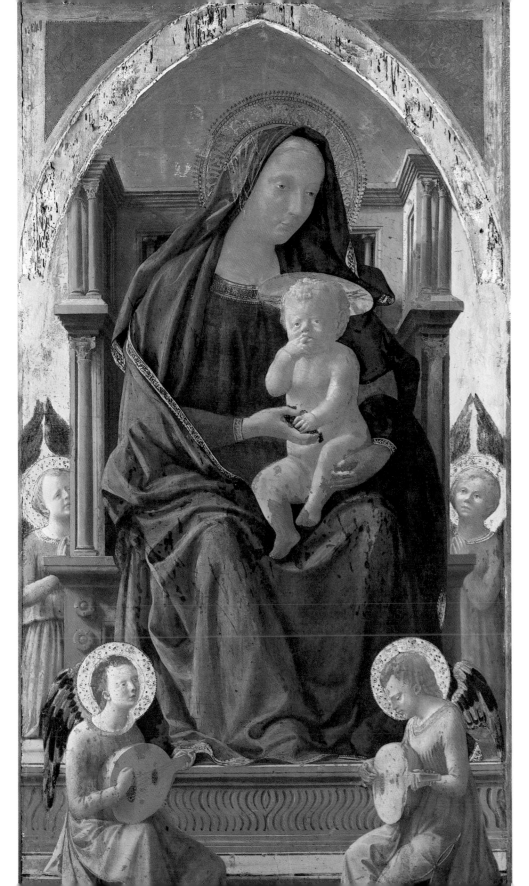

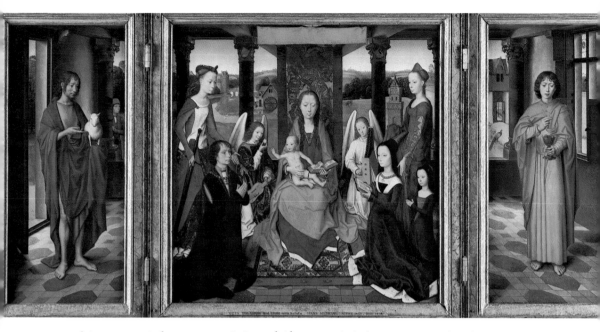

This picture is known as a 'triptych' because it is in three sections. It was painted in the second half of the fifteenth century for Sir John Donne, an English diplomat who visited Flanders several times during this period. He appears in the painting with his wife and daughter, kneeling at the feet of the Virgin Mary and the infant Jesus. Two male saints, John the Baptist and John the Evangelist, are shown in the outer panels, while St Catherine and St Barbara are included with attendant angels as part of the central group. One other figure, who may be the artist himself, peeps in on the scene through a window in the back wall.

The brightly coloured paintings on the inside of this small triptych may frequently have been hidden from view as, in some regions, they were opened only on special feast days, or during particular religious services. The grisaille paintings on the reverse of the wings depict statues of saints: Christopher, carrying the infant Jesus, and Anthony Abbot, standing in painted niches (11). The lack of colour allows the light and shade to create a convincing illusion of three dimensions. The bases of the statues even overlap the edges of their niches a little so they seem to extend out of the painting slightly, into real space.

10 Memlinc (active 1465, died 1494)
The Virgin and Child with Saints and Donors

12

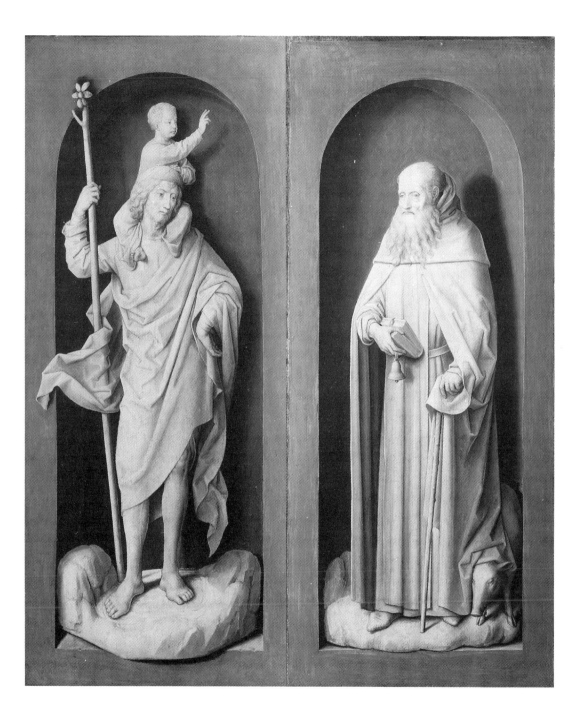

11 Memlinc
*St Christopher and St
Anthony Abbot*
(reverse of the wings of
The Virgin and Child)

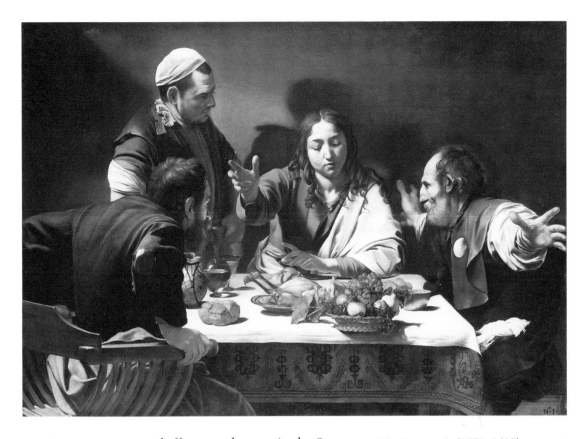

A more exaggerated effect may be seen in the *Supper at Emmaus* by Caravaggio (12). The innkeeper's distorted shadow is spread across the back wall, cutting off the space behind the figures and contrasting with the pale light on Jesus' face. Elsewhere, Caravaggio has suggested depth by the shadow below the basket of fruit and by the violent foreshortening of the arms of Christ and St Peter. But for me a favourite detail is the light on the elbow of the figure on the left. Not content with painting the arm so that it seems to be sticking out of the picture towards us, Caravaggio has drawn attention to it by allowing the man's white shirt to peep through a hole in his sleeve so that it catches a small but brilliant highlight.

Caravaggio has painted the exact moment at which the disciples recognized their companion. It was a miraculous moment in more ways than one. The disciples know Jesus died a few days before; yet here He is again, alive and well and performing another miracle – the blessing of the bread and wine, the

12 Caravaggio (1571–1610)
The Supper at Emmaus

13 Zurbarán (1598–1664)
St Francis in Meditation

14

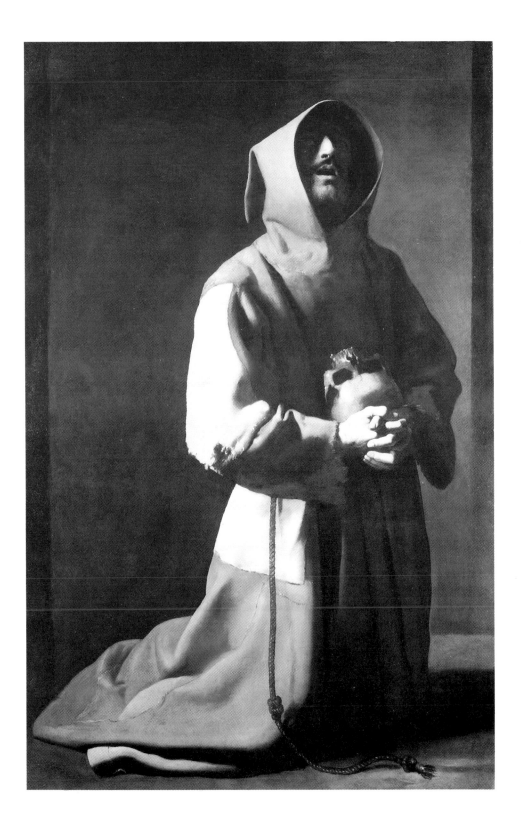

miracle at the centre of the Christian Mass. The light and shade in this painting do more than just create an illusion of depth – as if that is not remarkable enough, they also help to suggest the drama of the event.

A different kind of effect may be seen in the painting *St Francis in Meditation* by Zurbarán (13). The light and shade suggest an atmosphere of isolation and concentration rather than the momentary drama of a single miraculous act. The light comes from the left, casting dark shadows over much of the figure of St Francis. Though his eyes are hidden the direction of his gaze is implied by the angle of his head. Enough light falls on his clothes to show us the patches and frayed holes, which remind us that poverty is one of the vows taken by all Franciscans. He holds a human skull in his clenched hands, to focus his thoughts on death and his sins, and we can see nothing in his cell which might distract him from his prayers.

But think for a moment about where the light is coming from. Should the skull and the saint's hands be as bright as they are? Should they not be hidden by the shadow which falls on that side of the figure? Well, one of the nice things about being a painter is that you can be inconsistent if it suits your purpose. You can ignore the laws of physics and bend light round corners if by doing so it helps to create a mood or identify a character. St Francis was famous for the 'stigmata' – marks corresponding to the wounds of Christ on the Cross – that had appeared on his body. In this painting there is just enough light to reveal these marks, which distinguish him from any other Franciscan, but not enough to disturb the feeling of his isolation.

In the paintings we have looked at so far light has been used to produce a variety of effects. In *The Beach at Trouville* (14), it is the light itself that Monet is interested in, rather than how it might be harnessed to the description of solidity, or drama, or mood. The forms of the women's bodies dissolve in the glare of the sunlight and their faces flatten in the cold, grey shadows cast by their parasols.

Monet painted this little picture in 1870 while sitting on the beach with his wife. The light is recorded as

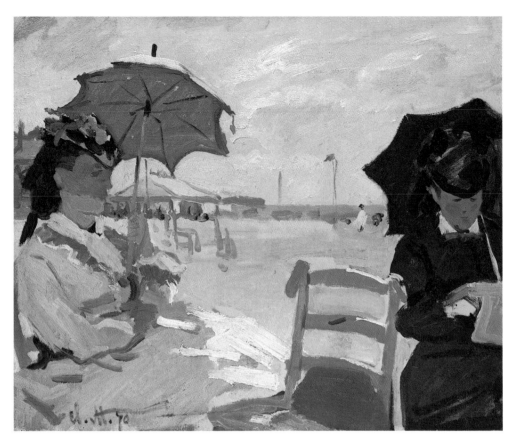

14 Monet (1840–1926)
The Beach at Trouville

accurately and directly as possible. Thick strokes of creamy white paint have been spread on to the canvas to describe the intensity of the sunlight as it falls on the dress of the lady on the left. Monet's intention was to record the light and shade at a particular place and at a particular moment, to provide anyone looking at the painting with an impression of the scene rather than a detailed description of it. The word 'Impressionist' is now the name by which he and other artists of similar interests are known, but it was originally used to criticize this lack of detail in Monet's paintings.

Contrasts of light and shade have continued to interest visual artists in the twentieth century. Abstract painters, who have no interest in any kind of figurative representation, have in many cases continued to exploit the effects to be gained by contrasting highlights and shadows. Even photographers and film makers, who have increasingly sophisticated techniques of colour reproduction at their disposal, constantly return to monochrome to obtain the effects of drama and atmosphere they desire.

17

Colour

At first glance *The Grote Kerk, Haarlem* by Saenredam (15) may seem to be painted entirely in shades of black and white, and you may wonder why it appears in this chapter rather than the previous one. In fact there are subtle passages of colour in the painting: delicate greys and blues, with touches of pale creamy yellow where the sunlight falls on the bare, plastered walls of the church. The colour of the three massive columns in the foreground contrasts with that of the wall beyond and emphasizes the distance in between.

15 Saenredam (1597–1665)
The Grote Kerk, Haarlem

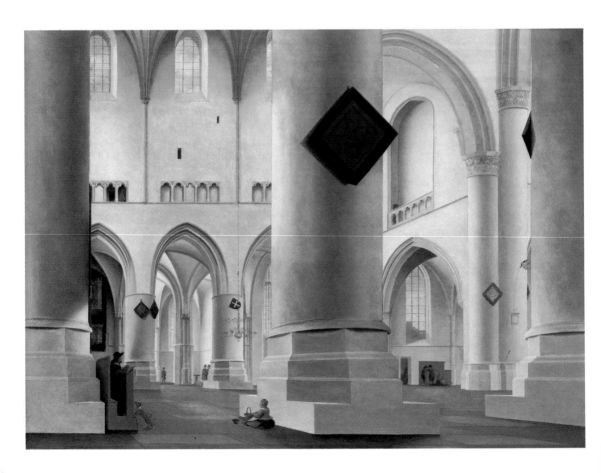

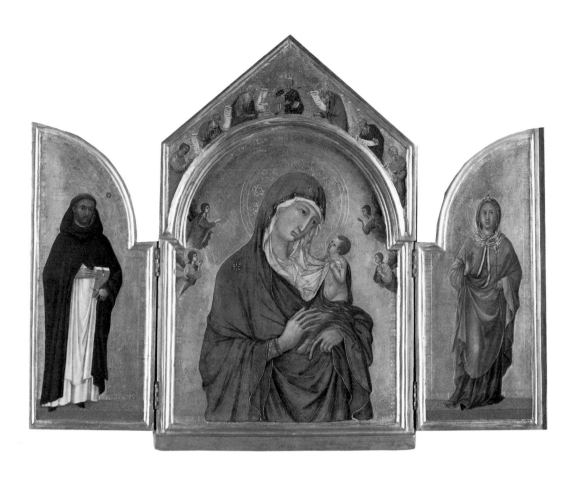

16 Duccio (active 1278, died 1318/19)
The Virgin and Child with Saints

In some paintings colour may be purely decorative, while in others it may add to the illusion of three dimensions or be a valuable means of dramatic expression. In paintings of religious subjects colour may also have a symbolic significance. For example, the Virgin Mary almost always wears the rich, deep blue we can see in Duccio's triptych *The Virgin and Child with Saints* (16). In the Book of Revelation at the end of the Bible, St John describes a vision in which he sees 'a great wonder in Heaven: a woman clothed with the sun, and the moon under her feet, and upon her head a crown of twelve stars', so it became traditional for artists to depict the Virgin Mary, the Queen of Heaven, dressed in blue, the colour of the sky.

However, blue was also associated with Mary for a very different reason. In the late Middle Ages the richest, most beautiful blue pigment available to artists was 'ultramarine', which as its name suggests, came from beyond the sea. This pigment was extracted from the semi-precious stone 'lapis lazuli' which was imported into Europe from the Middle East. The stone itself was expensive and the process of separating the pigment from the impurities was very complicated. So the blue paint which the artist ended up with was both rare and costly, and it was therefore reserved for very important people, and for the Virgin Mary in particular.

We can see just how rich and vibrant ultramarine was by comparing it to other blue pigments at the artist's disposal. In Titian's *Bacchus and Ariadne* (17) the

17 Titian (active about 1506, died 1576)
Bacchus and Ariadne

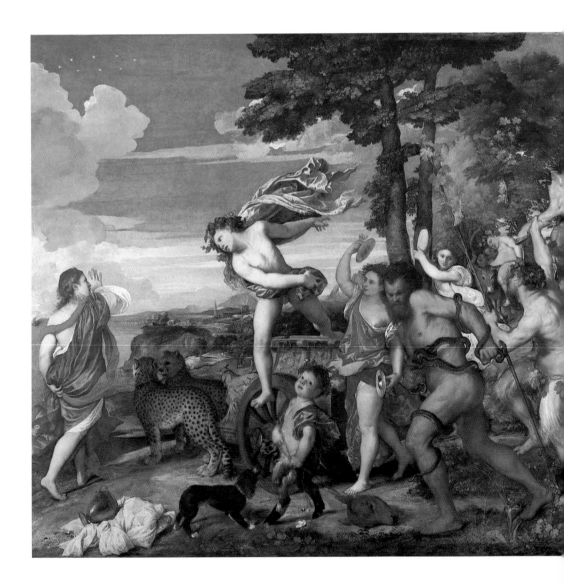

heroine, Ariadne, is shown running along the sea-shore in distress because her lover Theseus has deserted her. She wears a blue robe and is positioned against a blue sea. Nevertheless, she stands out distinctly because her robe is painted in ultramarine and the sea is in the less brilliant pigment, azurite. The bright red scarf also helps to separate her from the background.

The only other figure in the painting to wear this beautiful and expensive blue is the female dancing with the cymbals behind Bacchus' chariot. Ariadne and the cymbal-player are related to each other very clearly by this use of a common colour, but also, less obviously, by the fact that they are posed in almost exactly the same position. The only difference is that we see Ariadne from the back and Bacchus' follower from the front.

The rest of the painting is a splendid arrangement of sumptuous and subtle colours, including the exciting pink of Bacchus' cloak and the pale lemon of the cloth in the foreground. The landscape in which the figures are placed gradually becomes paler and bluer as it approaches the horizon. This effect, called 'aerial perspective' by Leonardo, occurs in nature and was much used by artists of this period.

Titian and his fellow Venetians were justly famous for their use of colour. Yet for a long time the richness and variety of the colour in this painting was obscured by a layer of discoloured varnish. When it was first suggested that this should be removed there was a public outcry; people were worried that the painting's warm golden atmosphere would be destroyed. But when the picture was cleaned its original colour scheme was again revealed in all its glory.

By the nineteenth century artists had access to a much larger range of pigments. Synthetic dyes were produced, many of which were permanent and not affected by changes in the atmosphere or by the passage of time. Scientists had also begun to investigate the way we perceive colours, and their research affected the way some artists used them.

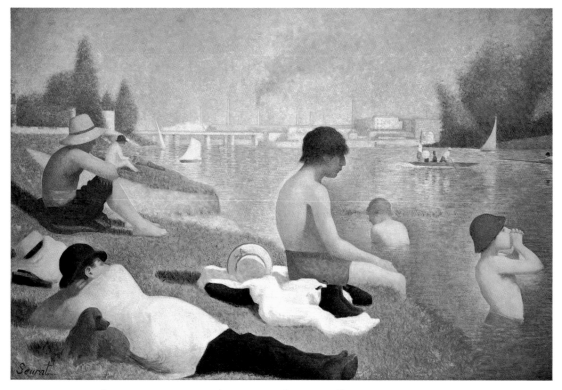

For example, Georges Seurat began to place small brushstrokes of pure unmixed colour side by side on his canvas so that they would lose none of their vividness. In his *Bathers at Asnières* (18) the image is built up in small criss-crossed strokes of brightly coloured paint. The separate dots and dashes are visible if we stand close to the painting, but they become focused into a more concrete image if we look at it from a distance.

It is a bit like looking at a colour television set: if we stand too close all we can see is a screen full of coloured dots. These are produced by a rather complicated process which exploits the way coloured lights react with each other. Coloured paints react rather differently. The 'primary colours' – red, blue, and yellow – cannot be produced by mixing any of the other colours in the spectrum. But the 'secondary colours' – green, orange and purple – are each made by combining two primaries (e.g. blue+yellow=green).

There is a third way of classifying colours, which is to pair one of the primaries with the secondary colour

18 Seurat (1859–1891)
Bathers at Asnières

22

19 Van Gogh (1853–1890)
Sunflowers

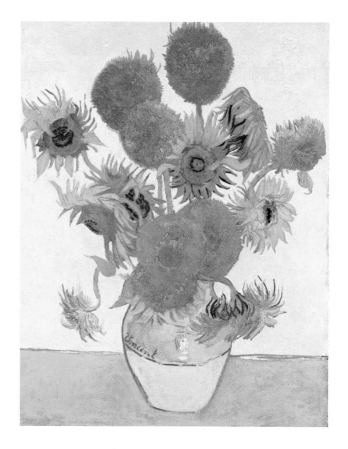

made by mixing the other two. These pairs are called 'complementary colours' and Seurat has used them together in many parts of this painting. For instance: the boy on the right wears an orange cap (made by mixing the primary colours red and yellow). If you stand close to the painting you can see blue dots in the shadow, blue being the third primary colour and the complementary of orange.

Seurat's experiments with colour interested many other artists of the late nineteenth century, including van Gogh. But van Gogh's use of colour is less systematic, more intuitive than Seurat's. He painted a series of *Sunflowers* in 1888 (19) to decorate a studio in the South of France which he intended to share with the painter Gauguin. In a letter to his brother he wrote, 'Instead of trying to reproduce exactly what I have before my eyes, I use colour more arbitrarily so as to express myself with more force.' This painting, with its strong oranges and yellows, is expressive of

23

the intense light and heat of the South of France, and of the enthusiasm with which the artist looked forward to working alongside Gauguin. But van Gogh suffered periods of mental instability and his optimism was short-lived. The painters quarrelled, van Gogh attacked Gauguin, and was eventually taken into care in a mental hospital.

Many artists of the twentieth century have interested themselves more in the abstract elements of picture making than in subject matter or content. People often see this as a traumatic break with tradition. But abstract painters and 'Old Masters' have more in common than you might think. They all use the same basic tools: colour, composition, light and shade, and others – like texture and line – that there has been no room to mention here. It always amazes me that with so many things to consider, so many possibilities, artists ever manage to finish their paintings at all. At the very least controlling all these elements is an impressive conjuring trick. At best the results can take your breath away.

20 Flemish School (around 1620)
Cognoscenti in a Room
hung with Pictures (detail)

II: THEMES AND SUBJECTS

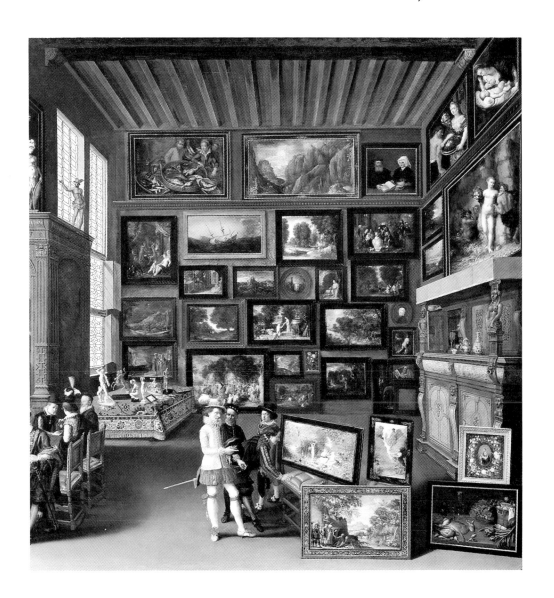

Narrative Painting _____

Y ou are probably accustomed to seeing pictures in
books and comics which present stories in
visual form. In this chapter we will be looking at
some of the methods painters have used to do the
same kind of thing.

In 1444 the artist Sassetta delivered an altarpiece to
the church of St Francis in the Italian town of
Sansepolcro. The main panel showed St Francis
Triumphant, but there were also eight smaller panels
illustrating scenes from the saint's life. Seven of
these are now in the National Gallery. By separating
these scenes and representing each one on a different
panel Sassetta was able to depict them clearly and
without fear of confusing his audience.

My favourite shows *The Legend of the Wolf of
Gubbio* (21). This fearsome creature attacked anyone
foolish enough to pass through its territory – scat-
tered about in the woods we can see the bones and
dismembered bodies of those who tried to do so. St
Francis persuaded it to give up its violent ways, and,
in return, the inhabitants of the town agreed to
provide it with food. The saint and the wolf are
shown concluding this deal with a hand/paw-shake,
while a notary writes down the details of the
contract. The men of the town stand behind the saint
but keep well away from the wolf – they are eager to
see what is going on but wary in case it changes its
mind. The women too are keen to miss none of the
excitement as long as they can do so without risk to
life and limb. They look down on the scene from the
battlements of the city gate.

The unknown painter who is called the Master of the
Aachen Altarpiece made use of a rather different
technique in his painting of the *Crucifixion* (22). The

21 Sassetta (1392?–1450)
*The Legend of the Wolf of
Gubbio*

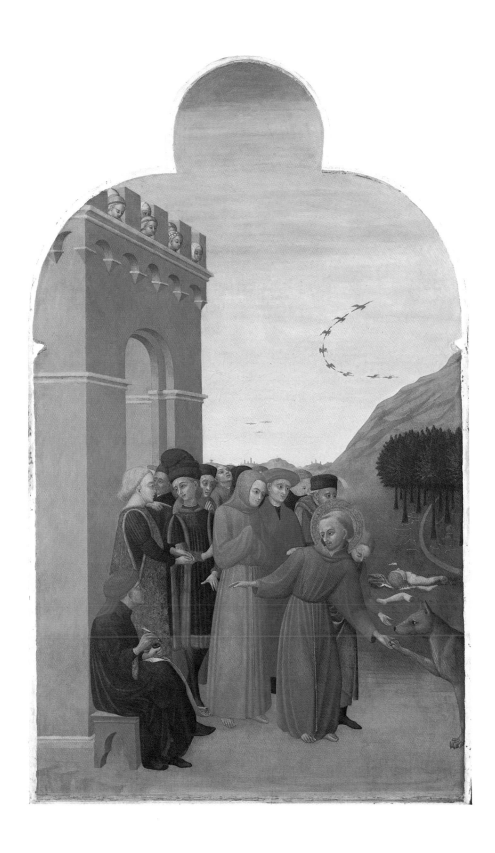

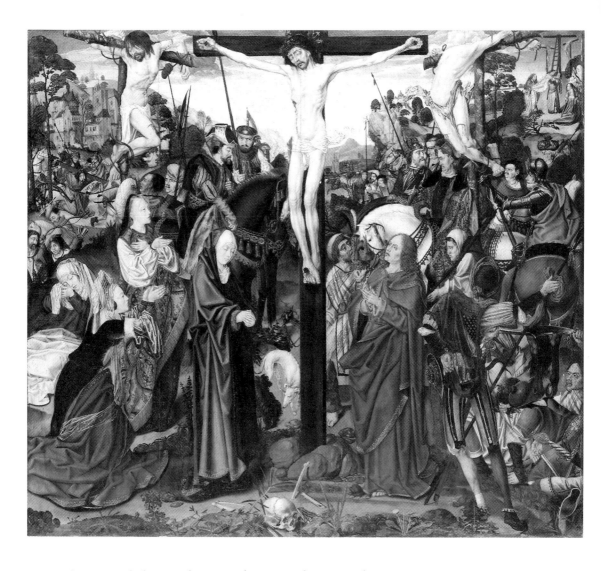

foreground shows Christ on the Cross, between the two thieves who were crucified at the same time. His Mother and one of His disciples, St John, stand beneath. In addition to these essential characters, the painter has included three grieving women on the left, and a group of unsympathetic soldiers casting dice for Christ's robe on the right, together with a selection of horsemen and curious bystanders.

However, the Crucifixion is not the only episode from Christ's Passion to be included in the painting. In the background, on the left, Jesus stumbles on the

22 The Master of the Aachen Altarpiece (active *c.*1495–*c.*1525) *The Crucifixion*

road to Calvary, and on the right, His body has been taken down from the Cross and is being carried away to the tomb.

These episodes took place, of course, one after the other over a period of time. The artist has attempted to suggest this passage of time by placing the scenes next to each other so that they may be 'read' in the right order, from left to right. The landscape in which they are set flows continuously around them, and the anonymous figures help to bridge the spaces in between. The artist has combined several parts of the story in one painting, but concentrates our attention on the most important of them: the Crucifixion.

In fact this picture was originally the centre panel of a triptych, the wings of which are now in the main art gallery in Liverpool. Like the centre panel each of the wings depicts one main event, with other scenes from the story in the background. So the painting in its original form would have illustrated the full story of Christ's Passion and Death.

Of course, storytelling is not simply a matter of describing events. A good storyteller can breathe excitement, drama and atmosphere into his tale, and engage our sympathy for his characters. The story referred to in Claude's 'Enchanted Castle' (23) is as complicated as a television soap-opera: the woman is

23 Claude (1604/5?–1682) *'The Enchanted Castle'*

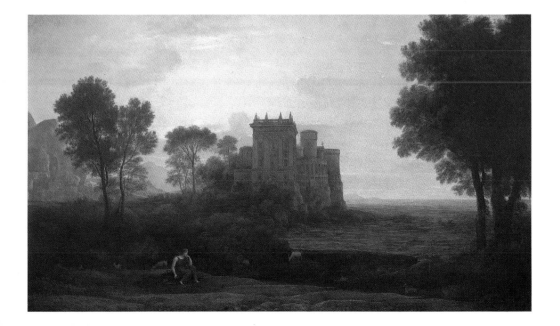

Psyche, whose lover Cupid lives in the castle from which she has been excluded by Cupid's jealous mother, Venus. But we are shown very few of these narrative details in the painting. All we see is a young woman sitting near an impregnable fortress, in a rather sombre landscape. The artist has concentrated on the general atmosphere of mystery and melancholy, rather than cluttering the scene with particularities of character or plot. Enchantment is suggested not by a lot of surreal or fantastic details, but by the fairytale castle which rises close to the water's edge and by the use of light and colour.

In *Perseus turning Phineas and his Followers to Stone* (24), Luca Giordano has attempted to convey the frantic movement and drama of this terrifying story. Perseus, having killed the Gorgon Medusa and rescued the princess Andromeda from the clutches of a sea monster, then had to fight Phineas for her hand in marriage. The painting shows us the point at which Phineas and his followers are being turned to stone by Medusa's petrifying gaze.

Giordano has created a stage-like space, with a draped curtain above it and wings on either side. The palace walls and stacked serving dishes look insubstantial, as if they are painted on a theatrical backdrop. Beams of light stream in, like spotlights, from the top left-hand corner, while the spilt wine and the blood trickle downwards towards the spectator as if the floor is sloping, like a stage towards an auditorium. The painting may not depict any specific theatrical performance; whether Giordano ever saw a play based on this story is neither here nor there. What is interesting is the way in which he incorporates theatrical lighting and other details into a static painted image. By using cold greys and warm flesh tones the artist has even managed to suggest a kind of theatrical special effect – the followers of Phineas have not been turned to stone in a single terrifying second, it is happening this very minute before our eyes.

The legend of Perseus is never dull, but the artist has depicted one of the most exciting sections of it and conveyed the excitement along with the story.

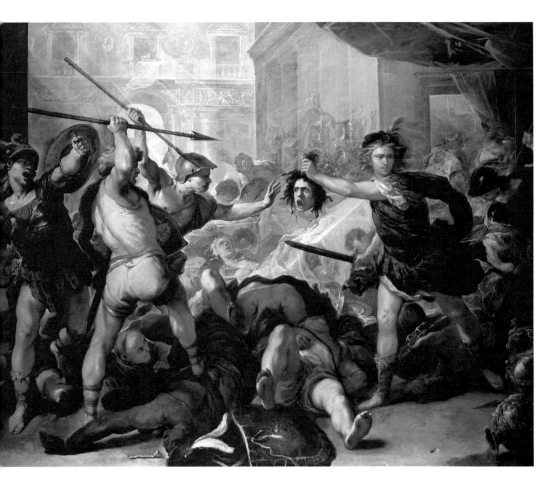

24 Giordano (1634–1705)
Perseus turning Phineas and his Followers to Stone

The theatre is also referred to in the *Scene from 'The Forcibly Bewitched'* by Goya (25). The painting illustrates an episode from a comedy written by the Spanish playwright Antonio de Zamora, which was first performed in 1698. The central character, Don Claudio, has been told that he will die if he allows the little lamp to go out, and he is shown filling it up with oil to keep it alight. Goya may have seen a production of the play at the theatre and this might have suggested the rather unusual composition of the painting.

However, he has not been content simply to illustrate the story: he has also included the corner of a book or a theatre programme on which fragments of the play's opening line appear. By this simple device the artist has placed us, the spectators, in the position of the members of a theatre audience.

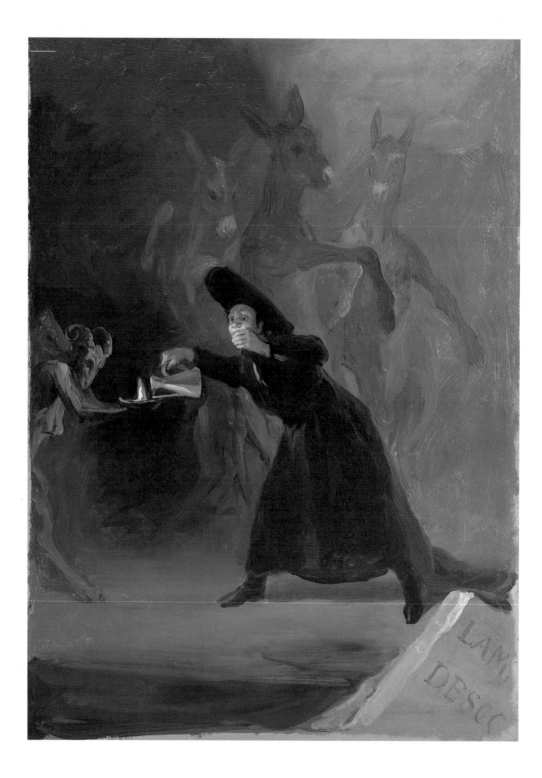

25 Goya (1746–1828)
Scene from 'The Forcibly Bewitched'

He has also been able to convey some of the play's farcical melodrama. The restricted lighting and subdued colour suggest an atmosphere of mystery and suspense that is highly appropriate to this particular point in the play. They also make it difficult for Don Claudio (and for us) to decide whether the grotesque creatures we can see in the gloom are real or merely inventions of the character's imagination. On the other hand, the worried expression on the man's face is overdone to the point of absurdity, to suggest that nothing really serious is going to happen to him in the end. The method of hinting at narrative and mood used by Goya in this painting is ingenious and very effective.

The Nude

When I was an art student I was required to pay regular visits to a life-drawing studio. There a nude model would pose on a raised platform so that aspiring artists like myself could study the anatomy and proportions of the human figure from life. For many people drawing the nude is just a technical exercise, but not all paintings and drawings of the subject are as objective and unemotional as those produced in a life-class. Artists, like the rest of us, may find the naked body exciting, embarrassing, shocking or amusing, and they may express any of these feelings in their paintings.

In Europe in the thirteenth century, the Church was the major patron of the visual arts. Painters were commissioned to produce large-scale altarpieces and smaller devotional works, and to decorate churches with scenes from the lives of Jesus and the saints. In circumstances like these the naked body was rarely seen in a positive light. Nudity was more often thought of as shocking or humiliating. For example, Jesus could be shown comfortably without clothes as a baby or at His Baptism, but being stripped was one of the ways in which He was humiliated by the Romans before His Crucifixion. Just how much humiliation He endured can be seen in paintings like the *Crucifix* by the Master of St Francis (26).

Here the nearly naked body is twisted in agony so that the chest and rib-cage only vaguely resemble the real forms of the male torso. The drawing of the figure conforms to a traditional pattern which the artist may have learned from other paintings. Of course, he may also have used his own body as a model, but the use of other living models would have been frowned upon by the Church at this time.

26 The Master of St Francis (active late 13th century) *Crucifix*

34

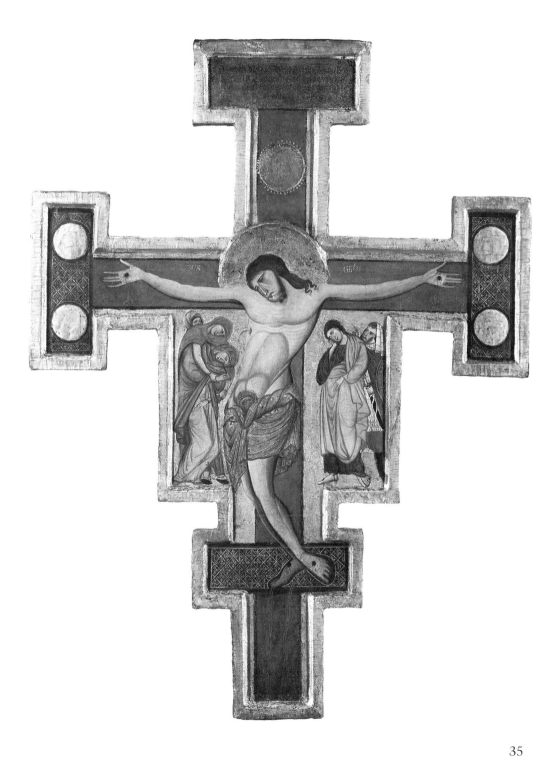

By the fifteenth century the Church's attitude to nudity had relaxed, but only slightly. Artists were beginning to use living models at least for their male figures, and some even pursued the study of anatomy to the point of dissecting corpses, though these dissections were conducted under conditions of great secrecy as the penalties for desecrating the bodies of the dead were very severe.

The brothers Antonio and Piero del Pollaiuolo may have learned about anatomy by dissecting dead bodies or by drawing from living ones, and in *The Martyrdom of St Sebastian* (27) we can see how well they understood the body's mechanical structure. In every figure, veins stand out and muscles ripple with an accuracy which must be the result of observation. The saint himself is tied to a tree, almost naked, like Jesus on the Cross, or like an antique statue on a plinth. He must be in considerable pain as arrows pierce his flesh, yet the artists have chosen to place the emphasis not on his suffering but on the resignation with which he accepts it. He looks up to Heaven without flinching, confident that he will be joining God there at any moment.

St Sebastian was a Christian martyr, executed for his beliefs. But he was also a Roman who could be depicted in a way which recalled the classical past: we can see the ruins of a Roman arch in the background. It should not surprise us, then, that the subject became popular during the fifteenth century when artists and their patrons would have relished the opportunity of representing Christian virtues in classical forms.

If the male nude could be a muscular martyr or a suffering saint, the female nude was almost always associated with the pleasures of the flesh. Representations of Venus are very common in European painting, at least from the fifteenth century onwards. Before that time the Church would have disapproved of such a profane subject. But just as fashions in clothing change from age to age so do ideas about what is beautiful. Two very different views of female beauty may be seen in *The Judgement of Paris* by Rubens (28) and *Cupid complaining to Venus* by Cranach (29).

27 Antonio and Piero del Pollaiuolo
(c.1432–1498 and c.1441–1496)
The Martyrdom of St Sebastian

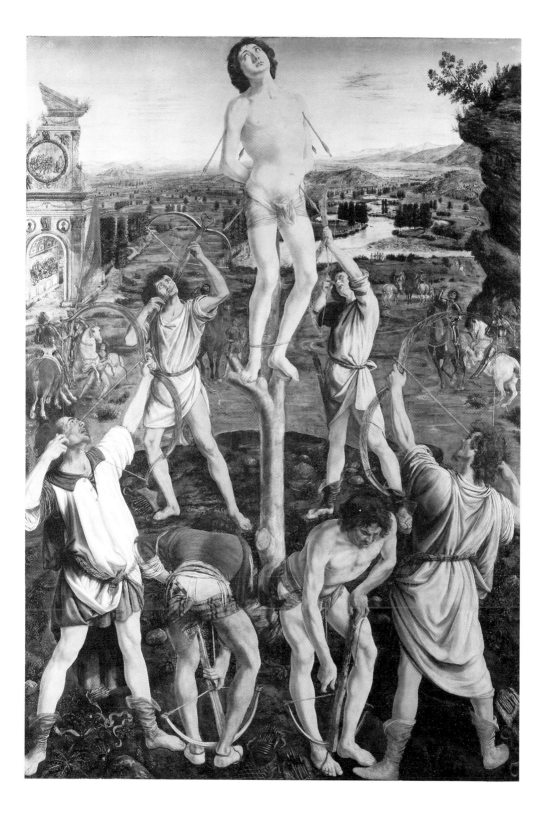

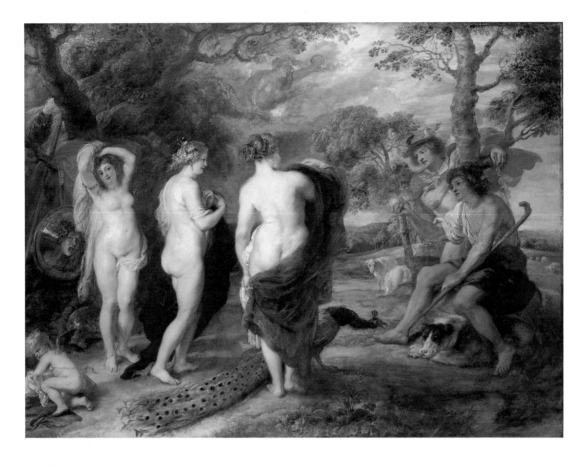

The goddesses painted by Rubens may seem to us rather overweight to be involved in a beauty contest, but the artist probably thought they were delightful. We know from portraits of his second wife that he was attracted to women of robust build. In fact he may have used his wife as the model for Venus, the blonde goddess in the centre who steps forward to receive the prize. The figures are posed so that we can look upon this particular type of female beauty from three different angles. By twentieth-century standards these women may not be very attractive, but their flesh is painted so skilfully that its softness and warmth are obvious even to people who find its abundance overpowering.

In the painting by Cranach, Venus is tall and slim, and she stands with her arm raised in a pose which shows off her naked body. She seems to be enjoying the fact that she is wearing only a silly hat which does

28 Rubens (1577–1640)
The Judgement of Paris

29 Cranach (1472–1553)
Cupid complaining to Venus

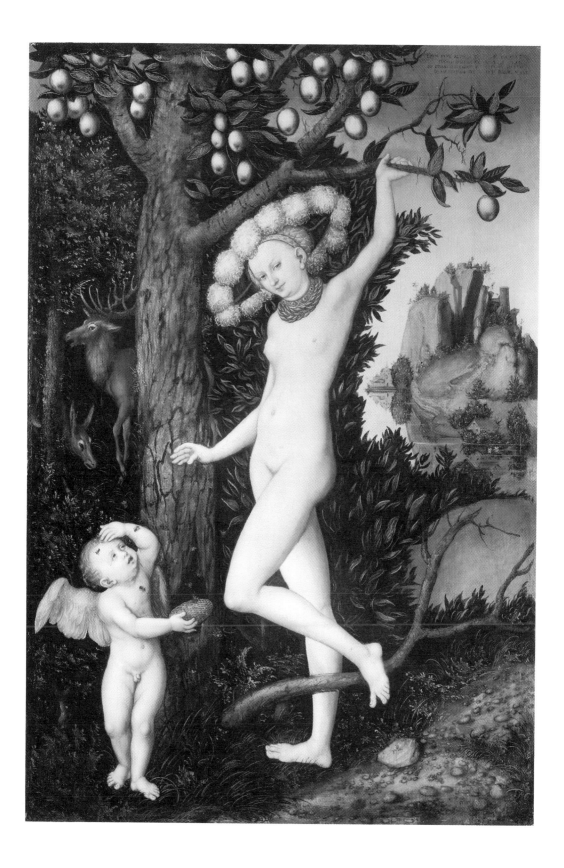

more to emphasize her nudity than to cover it. Cupid complains to her that he is being stung by bees, but Venus is unsympathetic. He should not have tried to steal the honeycomb in the first place, and anyway, she tells him, the pain caused by his arrows, which make people fall in love, can be much worse than that caused by the sting of a bee.

Occasionally, an image of female beauty manages to survive all changes in fashion. In *The Toilet of Venus* by Velázquez (30), known as the '*Rokeby Venus*' because it was once in a private collection in Rokeby, Yorkshire, we are shown a female nude whose beauty has been almost universally appreciated. She is young, healthy, not too slim and not too fat, and her figure is beautifully soft and rounded. The cool greys of the draperies on which she reclines contrast perfectly with her warm pink flesh, and the contours of her body are painted in soft focus, to suggest its delicate suppleness.

It is not clear exactly why Velázquez painted the '*Rokeby Venus*'; it is his only surviving female nude. But it seems to me that one of the purposes of a painting like this is to give the spectator a certain amount of sensual pleasure. We may think that obtaining this kind of pleasure from a picture is somehow wrong, or we may have become accustomed to machine-made images which can fulfil our desires in this direction more quickly and with more variety than paintings ever could. Whatever our opinion on the subject, paintings like this continue to attract admirers, though I sometimes wonder if people recognize their sensual qualities when they see them hanging in an art gallery. I hope so. It would be a great shame if such paintings were appreciated only for their accuracy or their technique, like the pictures produced in a life-class which may be anatomically correct but are rarely very exciting.

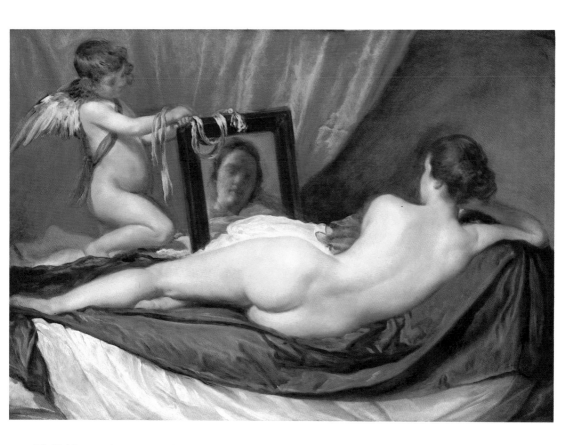

30 Velázquez (1599–1660)
The Toilet of Venus ('The Rokeby Venus')

Portraits

In certain societies the possession of a likeness of someone is supposed to endow the owner with supernatural powers over the person portrayed. The portraits we are going to look at here may not possess this kind of magical power, but they are all more than simply accurate likenesses. They may be intimate images or formal ones, but each of them tells us something significant about the sitter's character or position in society.

A particularly intimate portrait, one in which I think you can see that the artist knows the sitter very well, is Rubens' so-called *'Chapeau de Paille'* (31). This young woman may be wearing her best dress and her fanciest hat to have her picture painted but here there is none of the stilted formality you might expect to find in a grander portrait.

The picture was probably painted in the early 1620s and the sitter may have been Rubens' sister-in-law Susanna Lunden. The prominence of the ring on her finger may have something to do with the fact that she married her second husband in 1622. The pose the artist has chosen is reminiscent of the *Mona Lisa*; even the woman's expression, that uncertain ghost of a smile, reminds us of Leonardo's famous painting. But I think this picture is more approachable than the earlier one; artist and sitter seem more comfortable in each other's presence. Incidentally, the splendid hat is obviously not made of 'paille', i.e. straw, but of black felt. The painting may have acquired this misleading title because of some confusion over the French words 'feutre' (felt) and 'feurre' (straw).

By contrast with the *'Chapeau de Paille'*, *Charles I on Horseback* by van Dyck (32) is a very formal picture indeed. It may be a good likeness of a

31 Rubens (1577–1640) *Susanna Lunden (?) ('Le Chapeau de Paille')*

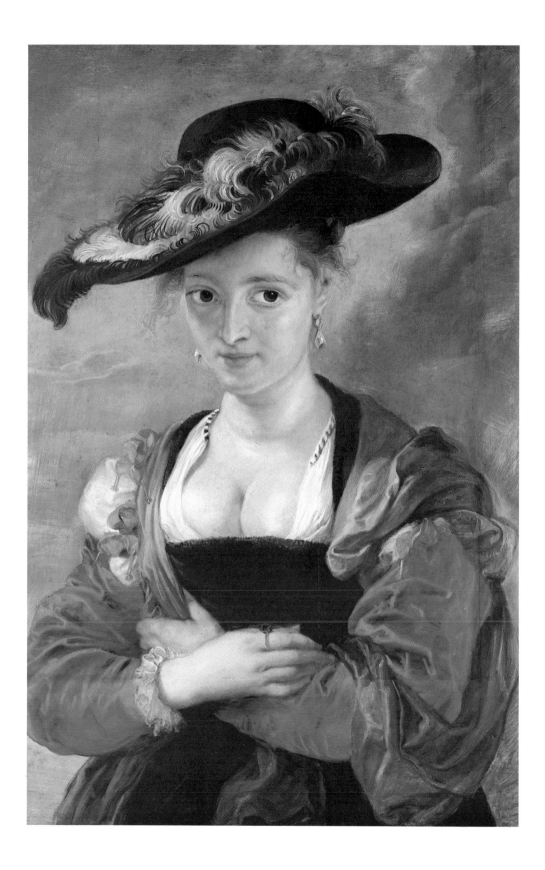

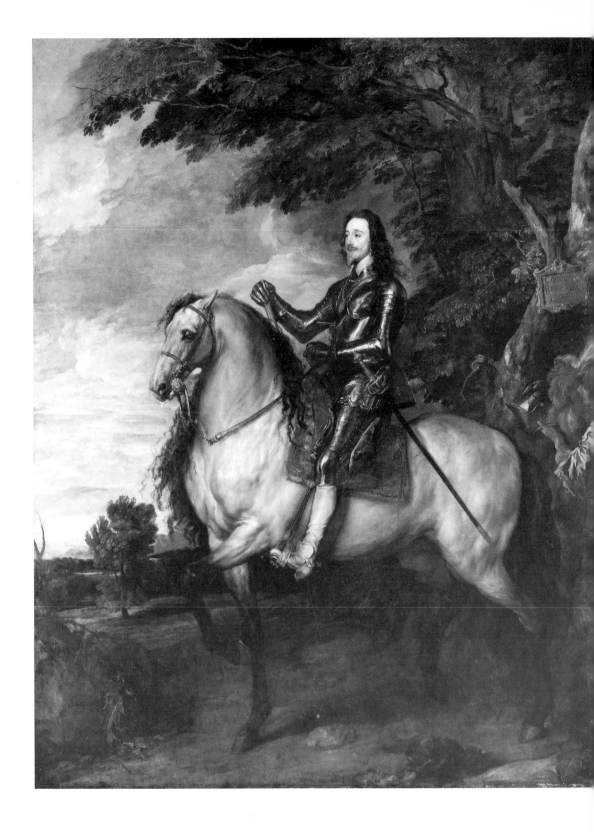

particular king but more importantly, it is an impressive image of kingship itself. Charles is shown dressed in shining armour, like a heroic knight of old, ready to fight if necessary and confident of acquitting himself well. His horse is huge and very muscular, but he controls it without even having to pull tightly on the reins. The king's gaze seems to be focused on the far distance, across the rolling English country-side of which he is the sole ruler.

This picture was painted for the king and may have been intended to hang in one of the royal palaces, where any visitor would have been greatly impressed by van Dyck's representation of regal strength. There is of course, no guarantee that the picture tells the truth. The artist may have been trying to flatter the king by investing his portrait with qualities the man himself did not possess.

Bellini's portrait of the *Doge Leonardo Loredan* (33) is another impressive portrait of a powerful ruler. He wears the cap and the embroidered gown which were the symbols of his office. But the painting is much smaller than the portrait of the English king, and the lined features of the sitter suggest, to me at least, a likeness which is realistic rather than flattering.

The head and shoulders of the doge are positioned above a kind of shelf on which a label bears the artist's name. This and the rather severe lighting enhance the portrait's sculptural qualities. Indeed, sculptured portraits like this were very popular at the period. The use of oil paint is also interesting. The technique was still in its infancy, yet Bellini uses it as if he has never used anything else: the tones of the face are built up in translucent glazes, while thicker opaque paint describes, in fact almost imitates, the threads of the embroidered costume. The overriding impression is one of quiet dignity and assured authority. Who can say whether these qualities were characteristic of Leonardo Loredan the man or merely of his office?

Goya's portrait of the *Duke of Wellington* (34) is another marvellous picture, rich in colour, superbly painted, in which the Iron Duke's strength and determination are evident from his expression. The

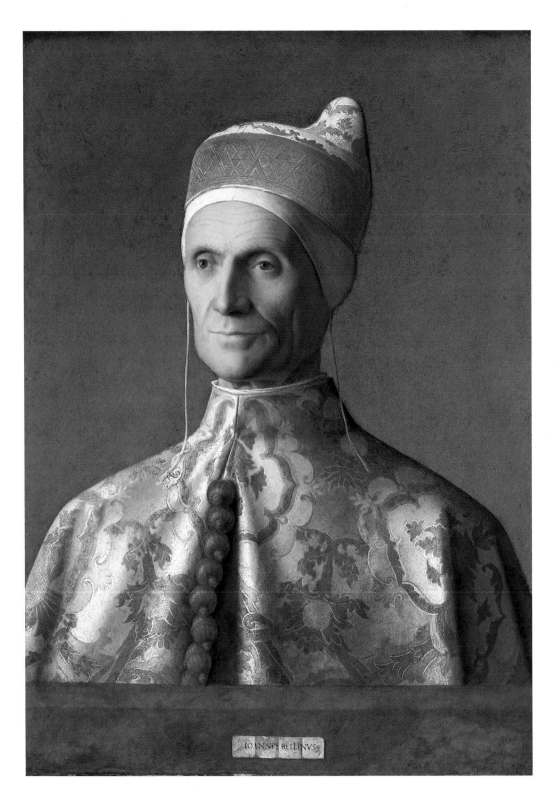
IOANNES BELLINVS

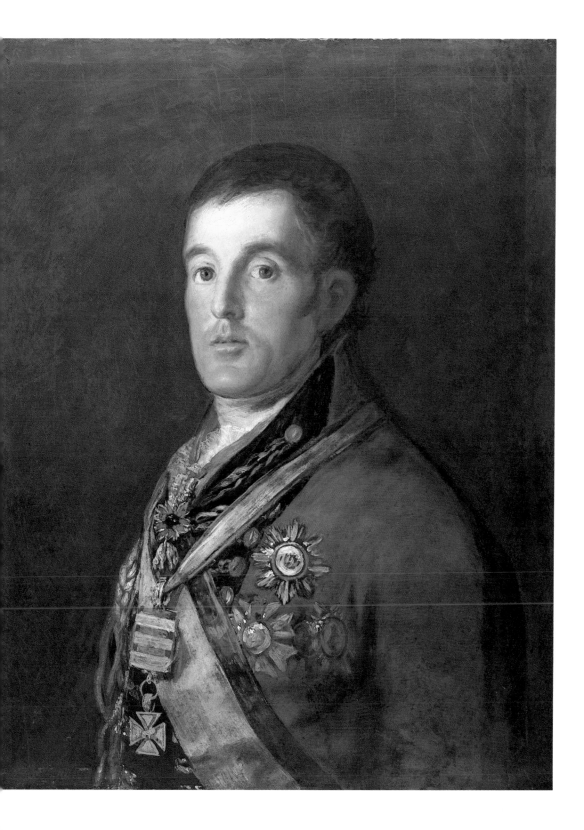

portrait was originally painted before Wellington was awarded the Order of the Golden Fleece, which he wears on a red ribbon around his neck. This and the Military Gold Cross below it were probably added by Goya when the duke returned to Madrid in 1814.

Goya had been Principal Painter to the King before Napoleon placed his brother Joseph on the Spanish throne in 1808. The French troops behaved savagely and performed acts of sickening violence which were depicted by Goya in a series of etchings called *The Disasters of War*. Although he also worked for Joseph Bonaparte, Goya would surely have been pleased to paint Wellington, whom many Spaniards welcomed as their liberator.

Finally, we should look at perhaps the most famous and certainly one of the most popular portraits in the National Gallery: *'The Arnolfini Marriage'* by Jan van Eyck (35). This remarkable painting functions on several levels. It is a splendid picture in which the textures of fur, lace, linen and velvet are superbly described. It acts as a record of the event, just as wedding photographs do nowadays. It may also be some kind of legal document, as the inscription 'Jan van Eyck was here 1434' on the back wall suggests.

Last but not least, the painting has a definite symbolic meaning. The man has raised his hand to swear an oath, the presence of the dog refers to the fidelity the couple are pledging to each other, and the single lighted candle may be intended to suggest the presence of God. The oranges on the sideboard may indicate the wealth of the couple and they may also be a symbol of the fruitfulness with which they would like their marriage to be blessed, something which is certainly referred to by the carving of St Margaret on the head of the bed (she is the patron saint of childbirth).

Of course, it does not really matter if we are unable to recognize all the implications of paintings like these. We may find them interesting as likenesses, because of their technique, or for any other reason. The point is that layers of significance like those we have mentioned here are present in most paintings and they may be easy to see if we take the trouble to look.

Preceding page:
34 Goya (1746–1828)
The Duke of Wellington

35 Van Eyck (active 1422, died 1441)
'The Arnolfini Marriage'

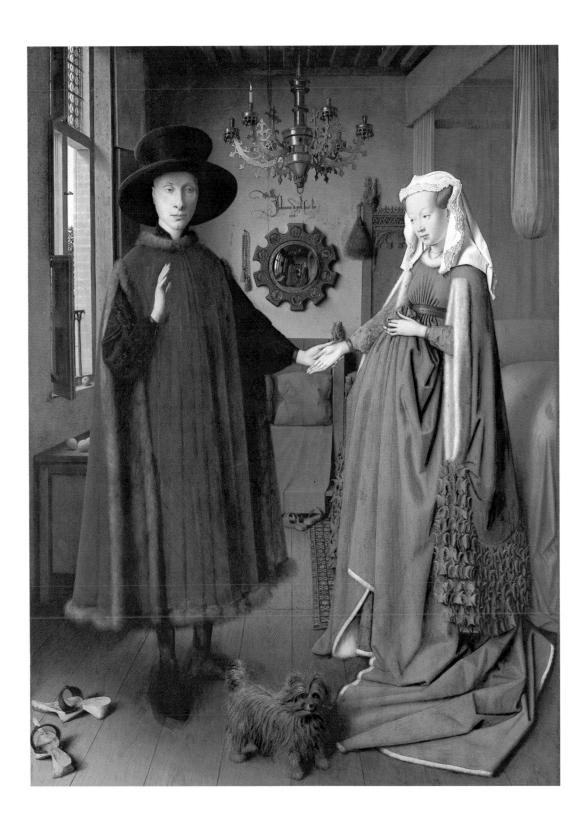

Landscape Painting _____

Probably the most famous painting in the National Gallery is a landscape: *The Hay Wain* by John Constable (36) seems to be everyone's idea of what rural England ought to look like. The picture has been reproduced so many times, and in so many strange places – on table-mats, posters for the Labour Party, and even, briefly, in a television commercial for a brand of English cheese – that it may be difficult to look at it with anything like fresh eyes.

36 Constable (1776–1837)
The Hay Wain

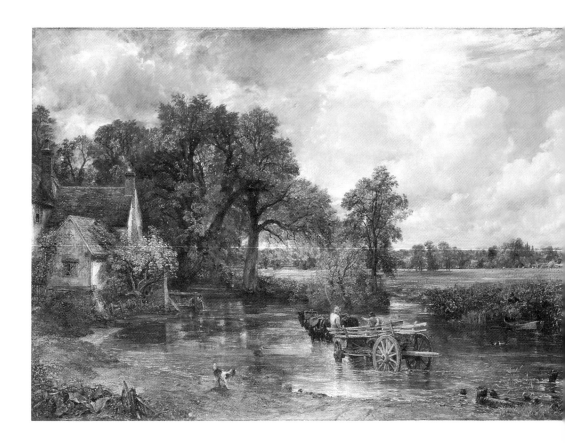

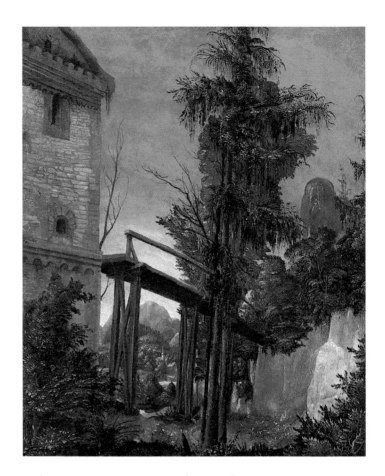

In fact, it is a great piece of naturalistic painting. A clear, bright light touches the white cottage walls, shimmers on the surface of the water, and shines on the clouds as they float by overhead. The colours are rich and fresh, as if the sun has suddenly appeared after a shower through a break in the clouds.

This bit of Suffolk looks much the same today as it did when Constable painted it. Yet the picture was not painted on the spot. Constable made small studies of the scene directly from nature but the final picture, which is over six feet wide, is a carefully executed piece of studio painting.

The idea that an artist could paint a stretch of countryside directly from nature, without modifying it or tidying it up in any way, became common in the West only in the last century. In fact, although there are some ancient examples of landscape painting, the

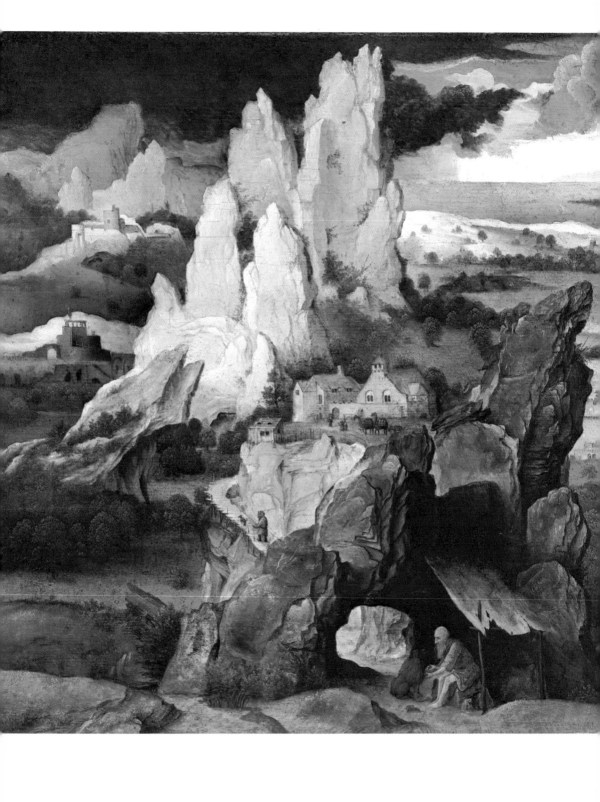

38 Attributed to Patenier
(active 1515, died not later
than 1524)
*St Jerome in a Rocky
Landscape*

subject only really became popular relatively recently. One of the earliest painters to demonstrate an interest in the subject for its own sake was Albrecht Altdorfer who painted *Landscape with a Footbridge* (37) in about 1520. In pictures like this Altdorfer virtually invented a new type of painting; there were no traditions from which he could learn. In spite of this, or maybe because of it, his painting is as convincing as a view through a window would be.

Though it was painted at about the same time, the picture of *St Jerome in a Rocky Landscape*, attributed to Joachim Patenier (38), is as fantastic as the Altdorfer is naturalistic. The saint is shown taking the thorn out of a lion's paw, but the artist is more interested in the amazing landscape of jagged rocks and steeply rising cliffs. It is uncomfortable and unwelcoming. Even the sky is threatening.

I can remember looking at this painting in reproduction long before I ever saw the real thing, and though I knew it was small it still came as something of a shock when I realized exactly how small it is: less than 15 inches high. It remains a powerful image despite its tiny size.

The landscape also dominates in Claude's *Marriage of Isaac and Rebekah* (39), though the type of landscape in which Claude is interested is very different from Patenier's fantastic imaginings. Gracefully curving trees are grouped on either side of the open space in the centre. Highlights and shadows fall across the ground to lead our eyes from the foreground to the wood on the right. From there a path passes by the side of the lake and over the bridge to the trees and the mill in the middle distance.

Of course, this landscape, too, is invented rather than observed, and it bears no relation to the kind of countryside in which the event might have taken place. But the mood of the painting is calm and idyllic, and therefore appropriate to the story.

The countryside in Claude's painting is intelligently organized, not wild or uncontrolled like the real world often is. This idealized view of the natural world greatly influenced English painters of the

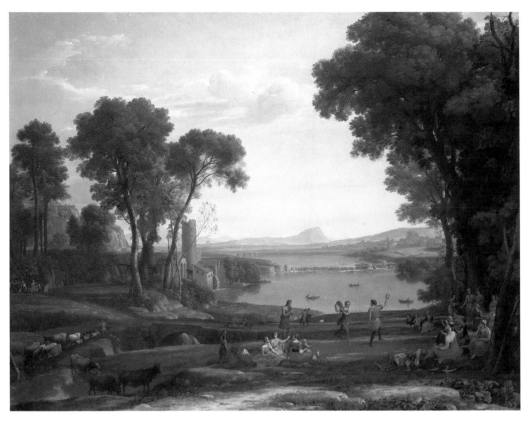

eighteenth and nineteenth centuries, and also the landscape gardeners who designed the parkland around many of England's most elegant stately homes. If you compare *The Hay Wain* with *The Marriage of Isaac and Rebekah*, you may get some idea of how unconventional Constable's picture must have looked to an audience accustomed to the refined paintings of Claude and his imitators.

I mentioned earlier that Constable made studies directly from nature, which he referred to later when working on his large paintings in the studio. Many people nowadays prefer these sketches to the finished works, which sometimes lack spontaneity. There used to be a world of difference between a preparatory sketch and a painting which was finished enough to be exhibited, but this distinction became blurred in the nineteenth century, when artists began painting finished pictures out of doors. By doing this they hoped to record the intensity of natural light as directly as possible. If that meant that the painting

39 Claude (1604/5?–1682)
The Marriage of Isaac and Rebekah

40 Pissarro (1830–1903)
View from Louveciennes

retained the spontaneity of a sketch then that was acceptable, even possibly desirable.

In his *View from Louveciennes*, for example (40), Pissarro has not tried to paint what he knows is there: every leaf and twig and blade of grass. Even if such a thing were possible the resulting picture would be difficult to look at; it would be a kaleidoscope of confusing details. Instead he has tried to paint only what he can see. Like his fellow Impressionist Claude Monet (see 14), Pissarro has tried to record the light, and the brightness or dullness of the colours in the landscape, so that anyone looking at the painting will understand exactly how the countryside looked at that particular moment.

Landscape painters may work directly from nature, indirectly from nature, or entirely from their imaginations. However, the process of painting any picture involves a certain amount of selecting and ordering of visual material. Even artists who profess to paint only what they find in the natural world constantly make decisions about what to include and what to omit. So no painting is ever truly a window on the world. The processes involved in making pictures inevitably intrude, even if the artist would prefer them not to.

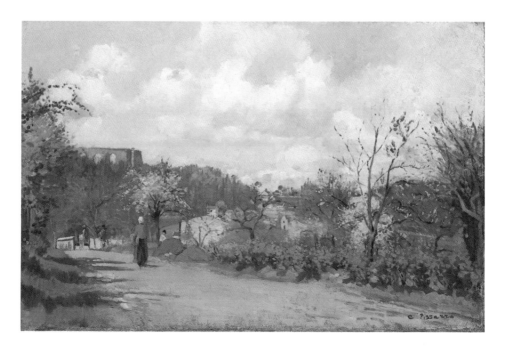

Still-life _____

A still-life is an arrangement of inanimate objects (the term comes from the Dutch phrase 'still-leven'). The objects in a painted still-life may have been selected simply because the artist found them visually interesting. Alternatively, the artist may have chosen certain objects for their symbolic meanings. For example, to you and me a clock may be nothing more than a machine which tells us the time, but to someone living in the seventeenth century it may have been a symbol of time itself. Similarly, an hour-glass in which sand drains from one globe into another may be an image not just of time, but of time running out.

A good example of conscious symbolism in a still-life is this *Allegory* by Steenwyck (41), in which every object has a definite meaning. For example, the books represent human knowledge; the shell, which would have been a great rarity in the seventeenth century, symbolizes worldly wealth; the musical instruments suggest the pleasures of the senses; and the Japanese sword represents earthly power. Originally the artist included another symbol of power in the painting: the bust of a Roman emperor, which was later painted out. The wine flask, which may be intended as a symbol of sensual pleasure, now stands in its place on the right, though the ghostly image of the emperor's face is just visible if you look carefully.

All the objects mentioned so far have referred to worldly preoccupations. The skull, the watch and the smoking lamp are symbols of more than worldly significance. They have been included to remind people looking at the painting that no matter how rich, powerful or learned they become, or how much time they devote to the pleasures of the senses, one of these days they will die and they will then have to

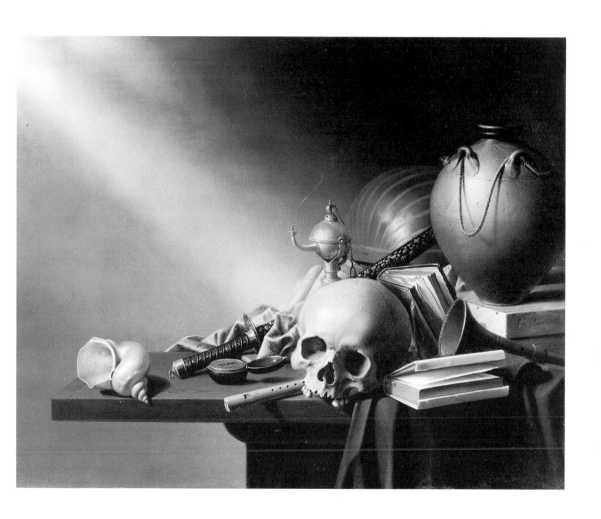

41 Steenwyck (1612–after
1655)
*Still-life: An Allegory of the
Vanities of Human Life*

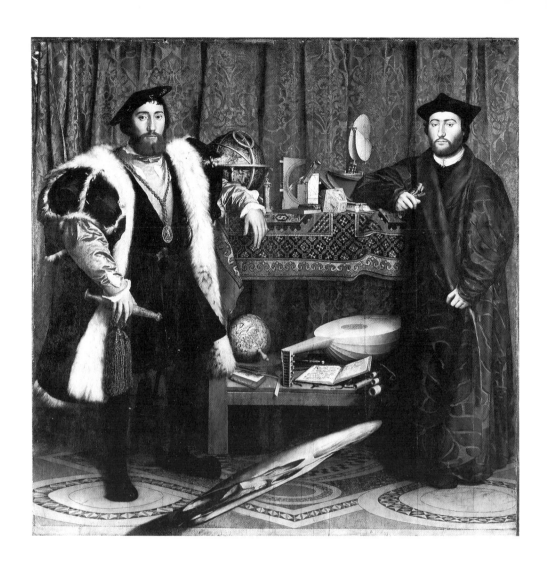

42 Holbein (1497/8–1543)
Jean de Dinteville and Georges de Selve ('The Ambassadors')

account for themselves elsewhere. When something is included in a picture as a reminder of death it is called a 'memento mori'. This interest in death may seem a bit macabre to us but until the early years of this century people were not shielded from death in the way most of us are nowadays. People may have been less squeamish about the hard facts of life and death in the seventeenth century because life expectancy was in many cases very limited.

Another human skull appears in the portrait of *Jean de Dinteville and Georges de Selve* (called 'The Ambassadors') by Holbein (42). It appears in a distorted form in the foreground, and can only really be recognized if the painting is looked at obliquely, from low down on the left or high up on the right. Many explanations of this extraordinary image have been put forward in the past: some people have suggested that Holbein may simply have been showing off; others maintain that the painting was designed to hang on a staircase, so that the skull might be recognized as one walks up or down. Whatever the reason for its distortion the skull remains a potent reminder of death and decay.

The other objects in the painting stand on shelves between the two men. On the upper shelf there is a quadrant, a celestial globe, and a number of other instruments which would have been used by contemporary travellers to navigate a course across relatively uncharted seas. On the lower shelf the objects refer to earthly pastimes: a lute, a case of flutes, and a music book which symbolize the delights of music and may be intended to imply a certain proficiency on the part of the men portrayed. In addition, we can see a maths book and a terrestrial globe on which the artist has marked the position of Dinteville's château in France. Finally, almost hidden behind the curtain in the top left-hand corner, there is a small Crucifix.

It is difficult to believe that these items were collected entirely at random. It is more likely that each of them tells us something about the men in the painting. We know what the skull suggests; the navigational instruments must be connected with the fact that the men are travellers (Dinteville was the French Ambassador to the court of Henry VIII).

The objects on the lower shelf probably refer to their interests or abilities. In fact the still-life tells us rather more about the men than do their faces or their expressions, which are rather inscrutable.

Courbet's *Still-life: Apples and Pomegranate* (43) might seem to be much less complicated. The fruit is piled high on a large platter, and painted directly in rich, warm colours. There are no frills here, and there seems to be no hidden meaning either. But from its date it seems likely that this picture was painted while Courbet was in prison, and people have suggested that the subdued lighting may be the darkness of a prison cell, and that the fruit may be a symbol of the world outside the prison walls.

In some paintings a still-life may occupy a relatively small part of the total surface but it can be so impressive that it dominates the picture. In the painting by Velázquez called *Kitchen Scene with Christ in the House of Martha and Mary* (44) the

43 Courbet (1819–1877)
Still-life: Apples and Pomegranate

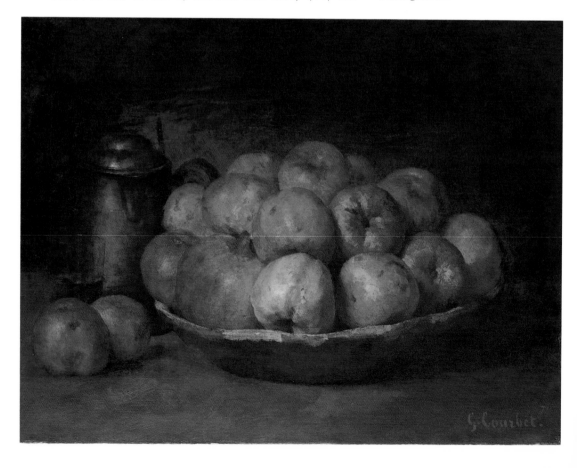

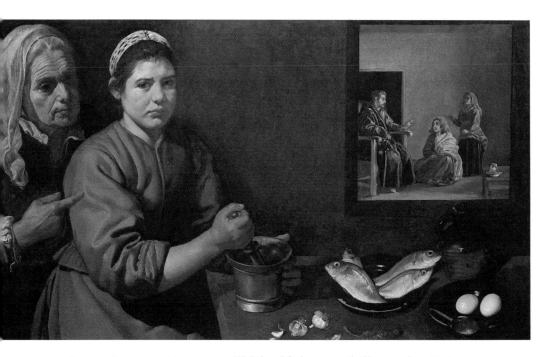

44 Velázquez (1599–1660)
Kitchen Scene with Christ in
the House of Martha and
Mary

still-life of fish, eggs, chillies and garlic is sumptuous-ly painted. For a long time it was not clear whether the New Testament story was visible through a hole in the wall or in a mirror; and there are still various opinions about whether the kitchen scene is sup-posed to be contemporary with the subject or with the artist and his audience. However, it is the still-life which concerns us here. The items the artist has selected may sound unexciting in the extreme, but the silver scaliness of the fish and the pearl-like surface of the eggs have been painted so lusciously that they make one's mouth water.

The still-life may of course, have some symbolic significance that we are unaware of, and while it is interesting to speculate about this it would be a shame if these speculations were to distract us from enjoying the picture for its own sake.

In the twentieth century artists have continued to paint still-lifes, though nowadays it is unusual to find them so concerned with symbolic content. Many painters have been more interested in formal problems. In his *Bowl of Fruit, Bottle and Violin* of 1914 (45), Picasso has tried to do more than merely show us what objects look like from one particular viewpoint.

61

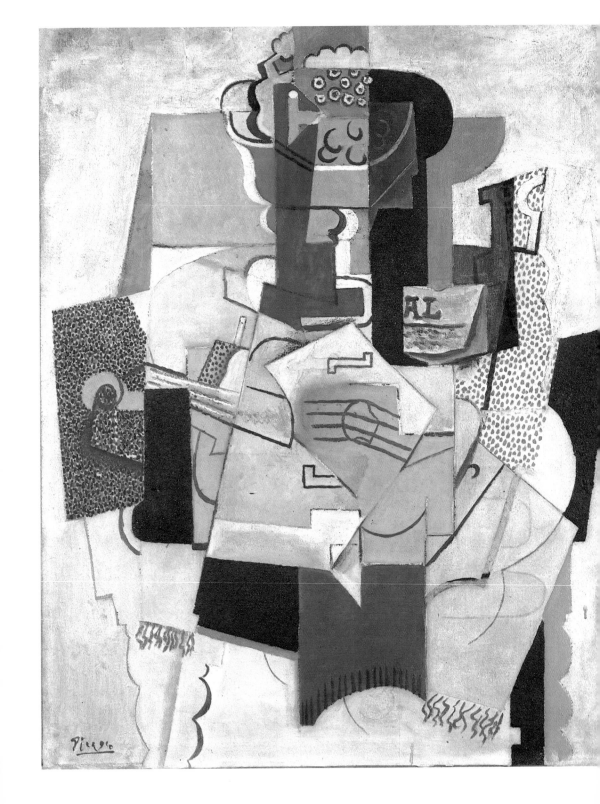

45 Picasso (1881–1973)
Bowl of Fruit,
Bottle and Violin

The forms of the musical instrument and the bowl of fruit have been fragmented; the table-cloth and its fringe are tilted into the same plane; even the fizz of the liquid in the bottle has been described in dots on the right-hand side. It is as if the artist has drawn parts of the still-life from a number of different angles and combined several of these views in his painting.

This still-life may look different from the others, but like them it demonstrates an interest in shape, texture, and arrangement of colour on a flat surface. It may be less easy to read but that does not mean that it is any less interesting.

III: PAINTINGS AND THE PUBLIC

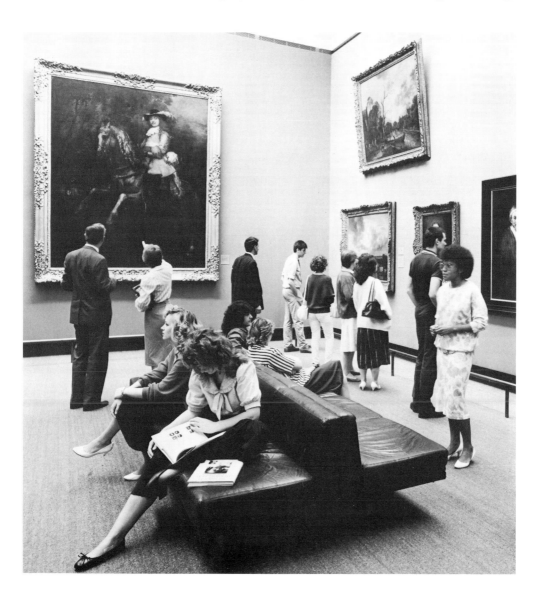

Past and Present _____

The pictures which now hang in the National Gallery are essentially the same as they were when they were painted; the *Annunciation, with St Emidius* by Crivelli (47), for example, looks much as it did in the Church of the Annunciation in the Italian town of Ascoli Piceno five hundred years ago, despite the fact that it has been transferred to canvas from its original panel. However, although the picture itself has not changed, a contemporary visitor to the Gallery may have a view of it which is totally different from that of a fifteenth-century Italian.

The painting depicts the Archangel Gabriel's visit to the Virgin Mary to announce that she has been chosen to become the Mother of Jesus. The ray of light and the white Dove symbolize the presence of the Holy Spirit; the apple and the gourd refer respectively to the Fall of Man and the Immaculate Conception through which Man may be redeemed.

These things would be appropriate in any painting of the Annunciation, but a number of the details in this picture have a special significance for the inhabitants of Ascoli Piceno. The figure kneeling next to Gabriel is St Emidius, the town's patron. He holds a model of Ascoli on his knee. The town's coat of arms and that of its bishop appear in the bottom corners of the painting.

And there is more. In 1482 the Pope granted Ascoli certain rights of self-government (the third coat of arms belongs to him, by the way). News of this event arrived in the town on 25 March, the Feast of the Annunciation, and Crivelli's altarpiece was commissioned to commemorate it. So, anyone living in Ascoli Piceno at that time would have recognized both the biblical story illustrated by the painting and

47 Crivelli (c.1430/5–c.1494)
The Annunciation, with St Emidius

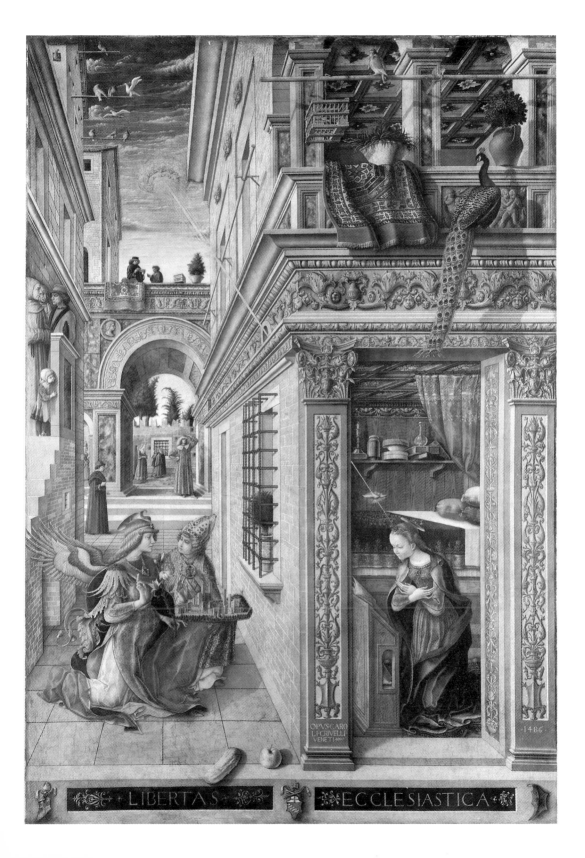

+ LIBERTAS + ECCLESIASTICA +

the political event it commemorates, as both would have been of vital importance to local people.

However, in 1811 the painting was moved to a public art gallery: the Brera in Milan. Anyone looking at it in these surroundings may have known about its original significance but would surely not have felt it so personally.

The painting was bought for the National Gallery in 1864. There it would have been seen by people so different in background and upbringing from fifteenth-century Italians that its various layers of meaning may have gone unnoticed. In the 1980s, most visitors know nothing about the picture's commemorative purpose and many would be unable to recognize its religious significance. They may see the painting as nothing more than an attractive visual image.

Some people think it would be better to exhibit paintings like this in more appropriate surroundings: in replicas of their original chapels, for example, to help people to understand their original purpose and effect. But placing a fifteenth-century painting in a contemporary setting will not necessarily enable a modern gallery visitor to see it with the eyes and sensibilities of a fifteenth-century Christian visiting a church. The way people react to a painting probably depends more on their education, taste and social circumstances than on the painting's physical environment.

The altarpiece (48) by Margarito of Arezzo, depicting *The Virgin and Child Enthroned*, is now hanging in the National Gallery with other Italian paintings of the thirteenth and fourteenth centuries. It arrived in the Gallery in 1857 when the works of Raphael and the other artists of the High Renaissance were regarded as the high point of Western European art. Margarito's picture, with its comic-like arrangement of narrative scenes, was thought to be crude and unsophisticated. It was acquired 'to show the barbarous state into which art had sunk even in Italy previously to its revival'. Well, times change. There are people nowadays who think of this painting as anything but unsophisticated, and who admire it

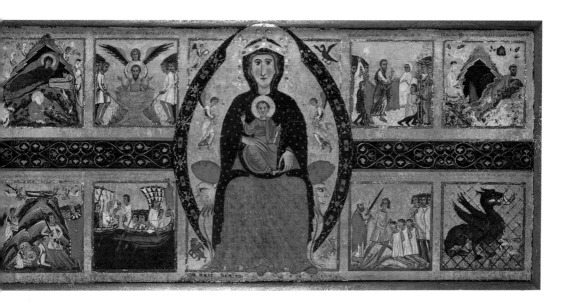

48 Margarito of Arezzo
(active 1262?)
*The Virgin and Child
Enthroned*

because of its directness and for the clear way in which it tells its story.

In the centre of the painting we can see the Virgin and Child enthroned in majesty. On either side there are scenes that illustrate episodes from a number of sacred stories. For example, *The Nativity* occupies the space in the top left-hand corner. Some of the other squares contain illustrations of stories which are less well-known to us nowadays than they would have been to the people for whom the picture was painted. But even if we no longer recognize the characters involved in *The Beheading of St Catherine* (bottom left) the painting leaves us in no doubt about what is happening to them.

A picture which still provokes strong reactions is Bronzino's *Allegory* (50), which was painted in Florence in the 1540s. Love and Beauty in the shape of Cupid and Venus are shown embracing, while Folly, Time and other less easily identifiable characters surround them. The precise significance of the painting is still the subject of scholarly discussion. But whatever its meaning may be the picture must have been designed to give sensual pleasure to the people who looked at it. It was acquired by the National Gallery during the Victorian era, when well brought up young ladies were thought likely to swoon at the sight of an undraped piano leg. At that

69

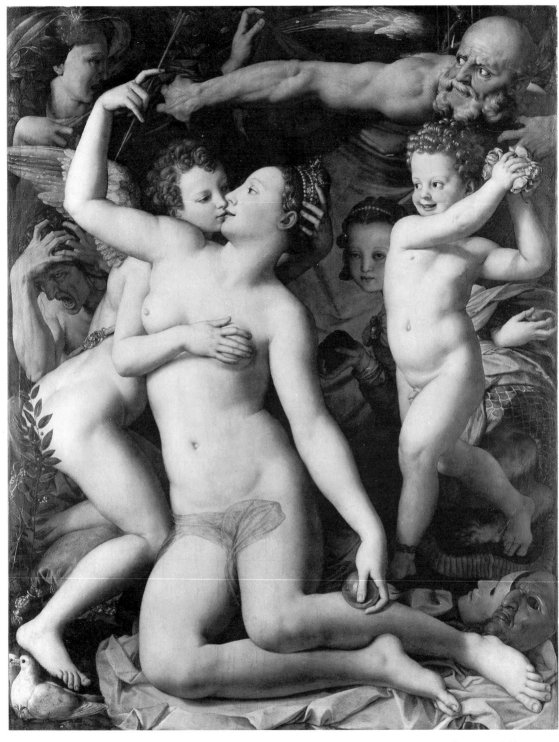

49 Bronzino (1503–1572)
An Allegory, before cleaning

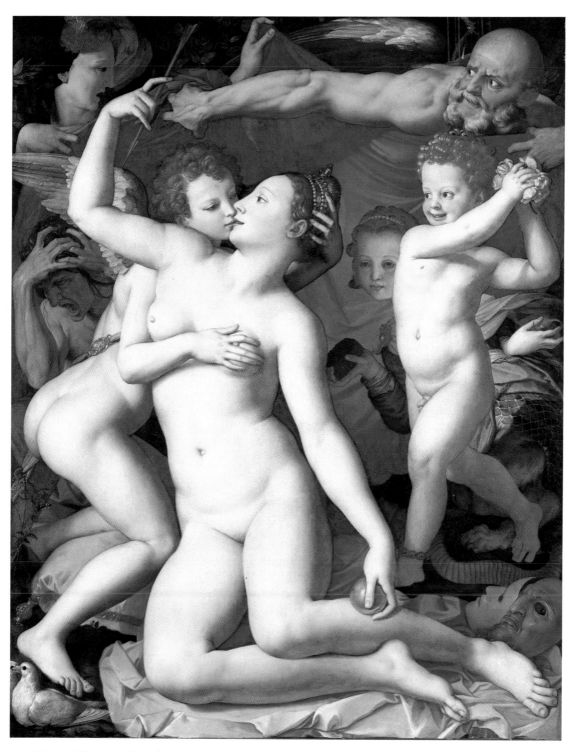

50 *An Allegory,* after cleaning,
with the overpainting removed

time the nudity of the figures and their explicit embrace would have shocked many Gallery visitors, and various parts of the picture had been painted out (49). Yet the Victorians recognized the quality of the painting and it was not hidden away or repainted.

The overpainting was removed in 1958, and though I am sure there are people even in the relatively liberal 1980s who would find this image too blatant for their liking, at least we can now see it more or less as the artist intended and decide for ourselves.

An artist's abilities are sometimes appreciated only after his death. Sadly, the reverse can also happen. While he was alive Delaroche was thought of with respect as an artist of high calibre. Nowadays he has been relegated to the rank of uninspired academic, a history painter who specialized in sentimental death scenes. Personally, I am quite fond of *The Execution of Lady Jane Grey* (51). It shows the young deposed queen just before her beheading, in a white under-skirt that emphasizes her innocence, surrounded by people who feel so sorry for her that they make us feel sorry for her too. Though it was made about 100 years earlier, it reminds me of a Hollywood movie of the 1940s, the kind they show on the television on Saturday afternoons. Paintings and films of this kind may seem a bit sentimental to us now, but they were made to conform to certain conventions. They were designed to appeal to a particular audience, and people still find them entertaining despite uncon-vincing sets and melodramatic acting. *The Execution of Lady Jane Grey* may not be a great work of art but that need not spoil our enjoyment of it.

Artists' reputations are bound to fluctuate with the passage of time, as each generation chooses its favourites from among the Old Masters. Perhaps if we realize this we will be less ready to dismiss painters whose work we find difficult to like. Their paintings may not be bad; they may just be tempor-arily out of fashion.

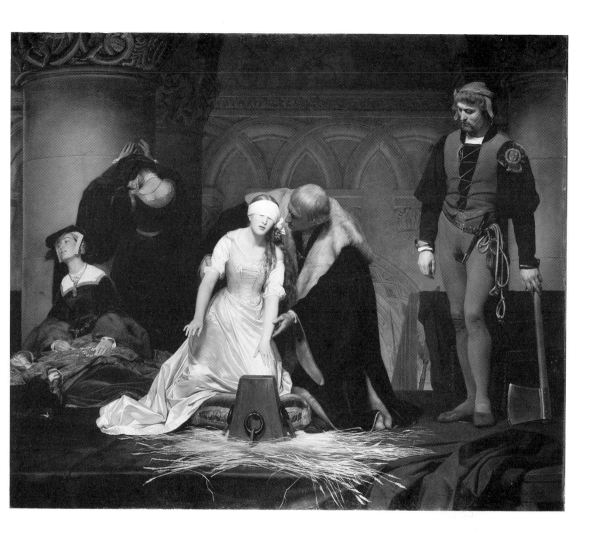

51 Delaroche (1795–1856)
*The Execution of Lady Jane
Grey*

The National Gallery Today _____

Originally museums were, literally, temples of the Muses, the ancient deities who inspired writers, musicians and performing artists. The word has since come to mean a place in which works of art or other items of interest are kept and displayed. The job of any museum or gallery is really just this: to acquire and preserve certain objects, and to display them so that people will enjoy visiting the museum and looking at the objects it contains.

The National Gallery houses the national collection of paintings by European artists of the past. It is run by a Board of Trustees who have various duties and are ultimately responsible for acquiring new works. In practice, the Trustees rely on the specialist advice given them by the Director and the curatorial staff, who are constantly researching their particular areas of interest.

The curators catalogue the paintings and try to find out as much about them as possible so that they can attribute a picture to a particular artist with a reasonable degree of accuracy. They trace a painting's 'provenance' (i.e. its place of origin and its subsequent whereabouts) and search for documentary evidence to prove where it came from, who painted it, when, why and for whom.

This is obviously easier to do with some paintings than with others. For example, Titian's *Bacchus and Ariadne* (17) is comparatively well documented. It was commissioned by the Duke of Ferarra, and it is mentioned in letters written to the Duke by his agent in Venice. On the other hand, the painting *St Jerome in a Rocky Landscape* (38) can only be 'ascribed' to Joachim Patenier. This small panel resembles other works by the artist but his authorship cannot be proved as there is no documentary evidence to support the attribution.

The curators need to keep up to date with the findings of their colleagues at home and abroad, and to publish the results of their own research either in academic journals or in the National Gallery catalogues. In addition, they may write books, arrange exhibitions and loans, and supervise the hanging of the paintings for which they are responsible.

An important part of any gallery's job is to protect and conserve its collection. Paintings are fragile things, sensitive to light, damp and atmospheric pollution. The only foolproof way to protect them would be to seal them in air-conditioned, light-tight vaults, but this is not a solution any public gallery could seriously consider.

The National Gallery employs highly trained people to clean and restore paintings, but the work of preservation is going on all the time, even while the paintings are on exhibition. There are low barriers positioned about two feet in front of the walls on which the paintings hang to prevent people from getting too near them, and security guards make sure visitors do not get close enough for any accidents.

The Gallery also tries to control the environment in which the paintings are kept. Light levels are monitored as too much natural light may cause the paintings to fade; and machines record the temperature and the humidity of the atmosphere so that the environment can be kept stable and appropriate to the contents of the room.

The staff of the Scientific Department analyse pigments and media so that when their colleagues in the Conservation studio start work on a painting they know as much as possible about the materials the artist used. Much of the work restorers have to do today involves repairing the damage done to paintings by their predecessors who had access to rather less accurate scientific information.

Once a painting arrives in the Conservation Department it may be cleaned and any flaking paint may be

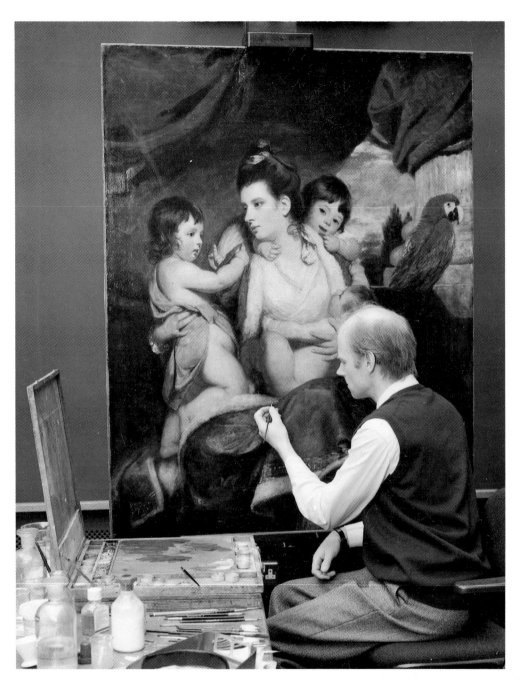

52 The Chief Restorer at work on *Lady Cockburn and her Three Eldest Sons* by Reynolds

fixed securely to the support (52). Then the surface may be varnished to protect it from direct contact with the air. The support itself may also need attention. Canvas may fray, tear or go mouldy. Wooden panels may warp, crack or become infested with woodworm. The restorers have ways of tackling all these problems.

Finally, the Gallery tries to make its collection accessible, to make visitors feel welcome and comfortable, and to inform them about the paintings if information is what they want. Paintings are grouped according to their period and place of origin and labelled clearly with the title, the name of the artist (if known) and perhaps a bit of information about the subject or the historical context.

In addition, there are guided tours and lectures for adults, and during the school holidays, quizzes, talks and other activities for children. During the term school parties may come for lectures or to use worksheets related to their studies, and they usually find that visiting a gallery is a very pleasant activity (53). In these and many other ways the National Gallery does all it can to encourage a strong interest in, and an enjoyment of, the paintings in its collection.

In the past you may have wondered why we keep all these paintings. I hope reading this book will have suggested a few of the reasons. We keep them because they are beautiful, interesting, irreplaceable and most of all because people get pleasure from looking at them. You may still think some of the paintings are strange or difficult to understand at first glance. But the more you look at them the more experienced you become at looking. You may find the habit grows on you, and looking at paintings may become for you the pleasurable activity it is for millions of people around the world. In any case, I hope the book has shown you that all paintings deserve more than a quick glance. There is always more to them than meets the eye.

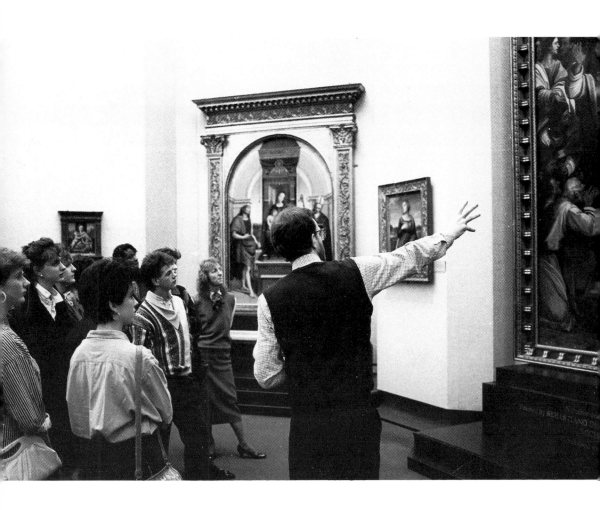

53 The author discussing
The Raising of Lazarus by
Sebastiano del Piombo with
a group of sixth-formers.

Further Reading —————

I f you enjoy looking at paintings and other works of art it is obviously a good idea to look at the real things whenever you can. There are local galleries, museums and houses all over the country that are well worth visiting.

However, if you want to read about artists and their work there are a number of books that you might enjoy. *The Story of Art* by E. H. Gombrich and *From Giotto to Cézanne* by Michael Levey both provide an interesting general introduction to the history of Western European art. If you would like to know more about how paintings are made you could look at *Techniques of the World's Great Painters* by Waldemar Januszczak and *The Craftsman's Handbook* by Cennino Cennini, which tells you what it was like to train as an artist in the fourteenth century.

The National Gallery also publishes other books that you may find useful. *The National Gallery Collection* by Michael Levey discusses a wide range of paintings in the Gallery and illustrates them in colour; the National Gallery Schools of Painting series has more detailed information about the most important pictures from every school – French, Dutch, Italian, etc.; and *The Illustrated General Catalogue* gives brief, factual information about every painting in the collection. Finally, *Myths and Legends* by Felicity Woolf, published in 1988, shows how artists used the classical stories in paintings.

Glossary

Aerial perspective
When objects are viewed from a great distance they may appear to be bluer than they really are and the contrasts of light and shade may be lessened due to the density of the atmosphere between them and the spectator. This effect is known as aerial perspective.

Allegory
A painting or a story in which the meaning is represented by the use of symbols and in which people personify particular characteristics.

Altarpiece
A painting which was originally intended to stand on or hang above an altar in a church or chapel.

Cartoon
A cartoon is a preparatory drawing in which the main lines of a composition are indicated. It is important for a cartoon (from the Italian word 'cartone' which means 'stiff paper') to be the same size as the painting to which it relates to make transferring the composition easier.

Chiaroscuro
Literally 'light–dark' in Italian. This word describes the contrasts of light and shade in paintings and drawings.

Complementary colours
Pairs of colours: red and green; blue and orange; yellow and purple. In each case the first is the primary colour and the second is the secondary colour made by combining the other two primaries.

Grisaille
A picture painted entirely in shades of black, white and grey.

Impressionist
The Impressionists were a group of painters, including Monet, Pissarro, Renoir and Sisley, who worked in France in the second half of the nineteenth century. Their name derives from the title of a painting by

80

Monet, *Impression: Sunrise*, which was displayed at their first group exhibition in 1874. They painted for the most part in the open air in an attempt to catch as directly as possible the effects of light in colour on their canvases.

Lapis lazuli
A semi-precious stone imported into Europe from the Middle East, from which a blue pigment is extracted to make ultramarine.

Medium
The substance – oil, egg, gum, etc. – which, when mixed with pigment, forms paint.

Memento mori
Literally 'a reminder of death'. Various objects such as human skulls and snuffed-out lamps appear in paintings as reminders of death. One famous example is the distorted skull in the foreground of Holbein's 'Ambassadors'.

Monochrome
A picture painted entirely in shades of one colour.

Pigment
The coloured substance which, when ground in oil or any other medium, forms paint.

Primary colours
Red, yellow and blue. These three colours cannot be produced by mixing any others but, in theory at least, all other colours can be obtained by combining two or more of them.

Provenance
This is a French word meaning the documented history of a painting. Art historians try to establish as complete a provenance as possible for a painting so as to attribute it correctly to a particular artist.

Secondary colours
Orange, green and purple. These colours are produced by combining two of the primary colours, i.e. orange=red+yellow, green=yellow+blue, and purple=blue+red.

Triptych
An altarpiece or other painting in three sections.

Ultramarine
A bright blue pigment extracted from the semi-precious stone lapis lazuli.

List of Illustrations _____

When we look at reproductions of paintings in a book it is useful to know how large or small the originals are. Included in the list below are the measurements, in centimetres, of all the paintings illustrated in this book. In each case the first figure is the height and the second the width of the painting.

16 Duccio (active 1278, died 1318/19)
The Virgin and Child with Saints
Wood, 41·9 × 16·5 cm; 61·3 × 39·1 cm; 41·9 × 15·9 cm
17 Titian (active about 1506, died 1576)
Bacchus and Ariadne
Canvas, 175·2 × 190·5 cm
18 Georges-Pierre Seurat (1859–1891)
Bathers at Asnières
Canvas, 201 × 300 cm
19 Vincent van Gogh (1853–1890)
Sunflowers
Canvas, 92·1 × 73 cm
20 Flemish School (around 1620)
Cognoscenti in a Room hung with Pictures (detail)
Wood, 95·9 × 123·5 cm
21 Sassetta (1392?–1450)
The Legend of the Wolf of Gubbio
Wood, 86·4 × 52·1 cm
22 The Master of the Aachen Altarpiece (active *c*.1495–*c*.1525)
The Crucifixion
Wood, 107·3 × 120·3 cm

23 Claude (1604/5?–1682)
'The Enchanted Castle'
Canvas, 87 × 151 cm
24 Luca Giordano (1634–1705)
Perseus turning Phineas and his Followers to Stone
Canvas, 285 × 366 cm
25 Francisco de Goya (1746–1828)
Scene from 'The Forcibly Bewitched'
Canvas, 42·5 × 30·8 cm
26 The Master of St Francis (active late 13th century)
Crucifix
Wood, 92·1 × 75 cm
27 Antonio and Piero del Pollaiuolo
(*c*.1432–1498 and *c*.1441–1496)
The Martyrdom of St Sebastian
Wood, 291.5 × 202·6 cm
28 Peter Paul Rubens (1577–1640)
The Judgement of Paris
Wood, 144·8 × 193·7 cm
29 Lucas Cranach the Elder (1472–1553)
Cupid complaining to Venus
Wood, 81·3 × 54·6 cm
30 Diego Velázquez (1599–1660)
The Toilet of Venus ('The Rokeby Venus')
Canvas, 122·5 × 177 cm
31 Peter Paul Rubens (1577–1640)
Susanna Lunden (?) ('Le Chapeau de Paille')
Wood, 79 × 54/54·6 cm
32 Anthony van Dyck (1599–1641)
Charles I on Horseback
Canvas, 367 × 292·1 cm
33 Giovanni Bellini (active *c*.1459, died 1516)
Doge Leonardo Loredan
Wood, 61·6 × 45·1 cm
34 Francisco de Goya (1746–1828)
The Duke of Wellington
Wood, 64·3 × 52·4 cm
35 Jan van Eyck (active 1422, died 1441)
'The Arnolfini Marriage'
Wood, 81·8 × 59.7 cm

Index

Numbers in italics refer to illustrations.

*Acknowledgements*_____

To begin with I would like to thank the teachers and school groups I meet every day at the National Gallery. Talking with students about the paintings in the Gallery's collection helped me to decide how to structure this book and gave me a clear idea of what to write.

In addition I would like to acknowledge with gratitude the assistance of a number of people inside the National Gallery. Sir Michael Levey and Alistair Smith read the text with great patience and made many invaluable suggestions, and my colleagues in the Education Department were constantly supportive while the book was being written. Finally, I must mention Sue Curnow and Lucy Trench of the Publications Department, who guided the book through the various stages of its production. I am very grateful indeed to them both.